PORTLAND
ROGUES GALLERY

PORTLAND

ROGUES GALLERY

A BAKER'S DOZEN ARRESTING CRIMINALS
FROM PORTLAND HISTORY

J. D. CHANDLER

AMERICA
THROUGH TIME®
ADDING COLOR TO AMERICAN HISTORY

The debt we owe to our ancestors must be paid to our children.

Abigail Scott Duniway

America Through Time is an imprint of Fonthill Media LLC
www.through-time.com
office@through-time.com

Published by Arcadia Publishing by arrangement with Fonthill Media LLC
For all general information, please contact Arcadia Publishing:
Telephone: 843-853-2070
Fax: 843-853-0044
E-mail: sales@arcadiapublishing.com
For customer service and orders:
Toll-Free 1-888-313-2665

www.arcadiapublishing.com

First published 2021

ISBN 978-1-63499-294-7

Typeset in 10pt on 13pt Sabon
Printed and bound in England

CONTENTS

1

NECESSARY ABILITIES

Any desperado with the necessary abilities could be elected City Marshal.

Eduoard Chambreau

James Lappeus had plenty of money when he arrived in Portland in 1852. He did not get it from his family, though. They pulled up stakes and followed him west a few years later. He got some money from selling his place, an establishment called Ten Mile House, in the California gold country, but he left in a hurry and might not have received full price for his goods or his business. No one knows for sure where his money came from, but there were rumors. Rumors dogged Jim Lappeus all his life, throwing shadows on his career and his achievements. There are some things we know for certain.

Lappeus was born sometime between 1828 and 1829 in upstate New York. In 1846, he enlisted in the New York Volunteers and sailed around the Horn to San Francisco. He was one of about 700 soldiers who landed at the Presidio in March 1847. Their mission was the occupation of the newly captured town, two months after the Treaty of Cahuenga ended the Mexican–American War in California. They would be disbursed over the newly conquered territory and mustered out in place.

San Francisco had only about 200 residents in July 1846 when marines and sailors from USS *Portsmouth* captured the Mexican village without firing a single shot in the "Battle of Yerba Buena." Lappeus and his comrades quadrupled the population when they landed eight months later. By 1850, after the discovery of gold on the American River, the city by the bay had more than 40,000 residents and the downtown area had been destroyed by fire four separate times. The lawless city offered many opportunities to get rich and the New York volunteers were in the right place at the right time to take advantage and become wealthy.

Lappeus, craving respectability, opened Ten Mile House in Sutter's New Helvetia colony and married Chloe Ann Burrows in the first wedding registered in Sacramento County. Ten Mile House was a "grocery" store, an early euphemism for saloon that was codified in Oregon law; whiskey was probably his biggest seller, right after the sex workers who were rumored to be available in his establishment at all hours of the day or night.

Left: James Lappeus was Portland's first chief of police and the city's first career law enforcement officer. (*Portland Police Historical Society*)

Below: San Francisco was captured without firing a shot by U.S. Marines and sailors from USS *Portsmouth* in the Battle of Yerba Buena in 1846. (*Library of Congress*)

VIEW OF SAN FRANCISCO, FORMERLY YERBA BUENA, IN 1846-7
BEFORE THE DISCOVERY OF GOLD

Times were hard in New Helvetia for the twenty-one-year-old veteran and his fifteen-year-old bride. In time, they had two little girls—Alida in August 1850 and Udora in October 1851—but both infants died in a smallpox epidemic in February 1852. The most enduring fortunes of the California Gold Rush were made by merchants who supplied the torrent of prospectors flooding the area. Ten Mile House prospered, but it soon had a reputation as a "sporting house" as Lappeus' lifelong fascination for gambling began to assert itself.

Later in his career, Lappeus exhibited a gift for straddling the line between legal and illegal conduct, but this talent was already developing before he left California. His nearest neighbor was Sam Brannan, first president of the Vigilance Committee; also, some of his best friends from the Army were members of the notorious Hounds gang that controlled San Francisco.

Officially the San Francisco Society of Regulators, the Hounds were led by NY volunteer officers in alliance with the secret Know Nothing Party. The Know Nothings, who would go public as the American Party, defended an anti-Catholic, anti-immigrant, white supremacist platform and were building a strong base in the post-Whig political world. The Hounds served as private police, enforcing a brutal protection racket. According to Eduoard Chambreau, a French–Canadian soldier of fortune who ran with the Hounds, the criminal gang was "dreaded because they were organized. They did pretty much as they pleased." Acting like a military unit, recruiters marched through the teeming neighborhoods beating drums and calling out young toughs to join the gang. "They enforced their will with military precision and it seemed like they couldn't be stopped," Chambreau said, "There was no security for life or property."

The Gold Rush drew crowds of prospectors from all over the world to the newly conquered territory. The white property owners feared the large Mexican population they now controlled, and Latino prospectors became the special prey of the Hounds. After attacking a settlement of Mexican and Chilean prospectors at Clark's Point in July 1849, a massacre that killed many, including women and children, the Hounds finally lost public support.

The San Francisco Committee of Vigilance was one of the earliest attempts to bring law enforcement and social order to California. Their first target was the Sydney Ducks, a violent band of misfit Irish convicts escaped from the Australian penal colony. The Ducks ran an arson gang in the fire-plagued city. The Vigilantes, although sworn "to do and perform every lawful act for the maintenance of law and order, and to sustain the laws when faithfully and properly administered," would not let anything stand in their way. Sam Brannan, Jim Lappeus' neighbor and leader of the 1851 vigilantes, was expelled from the Church of Latter-day Saints for the excesses of his committee. The vigilantes lynched four Duck members and ran the rest out of town. Then they turned their attention to the Hounds. Eduoard Chambreau vividly describes the breaking up of the gang and his flight up the American River to the gold country.

There is no evidence that Jim Lappeus was an associate of the Hounds; Chambreau calls him "our old friend" and visited Lappeus when he needed to lay low. Chambreau, a lifelong criminal/conman who was an active Christian evangelist when he wrote his memoir, has been accused of exaggeration, but some of his phrases lend authenticity to his story. For example, after describing how he helped Lappeus defend Ten Mile House against a large crowd, Chambreau observed, "Never throw a bottle at a man. It is an ugly weapon."

Lappeus and Chambreau were both wounded that night in April 1850 as they drove off the attackers with six-guns and whiskey bottles. Chambreau says it was "nip and tuck for a while," but Lappeus was "very determined, brave and true to his trust." Lappeus was probably opposed to the Hounds on political principles since he was a lifelong Democrat, but violence at his place and bad associates could not have endeared him to his neighbors. Chloe, seventeen years old and four months from giving birth, could not have been happy about her young husband being wounded at work. After his two daughters died in the epidemic of 1852 there was nothing to hold Jim and Chloe in California, and they took to the road.

The people who founded Portland, Oregon, envisioned and planned a large city, but it did not look like much in 1852 when Jim Lappeus and his young wife arrived. About a half mile of riverfront (from Captain Couch's busy covered wharf at the north end to the slaughterhouse and tannery in South Portland) contained fewer than 200 buildings going back from the river about 500 yards. Most of the buildings were box-like frame houses painted white with an occasional log cabin in the mix. Ambitious plans were in place for paving, but by this point, the streets, where they existed, were littered with mud holes. Businesses built crude wooden platforms to provide safe entrance to their shops, but they were slippery when wet, and with Portland's dreary weather, they were often wet.

The California House, above Skidmore's drugstore, provided luxurious accommodations and the services of New York-trained chef Peter Loudine for a daily rate equal to the average pay for a day of labor: $2.50. Jim and Chloe Lappeus did not have to worry about money, but if they had, there were four other hotels to choose from, as well as six boarding houses and some rental cabins available. There was also the Canton House, where Chinese visitors stayed, and everyone could sample popular, new, and exotic Chinese food. The fringes of the infant city were crowded with the temporary dwellings of Indians and other people who could not afford to pay a night's rent. The 1850 census counted 805 residents in Portland, but it neglected to count Indian, Asian, or transient residents. Since this population consistently doubled, the number of "permanent residents" the actual total is probably closer to *The Oregonian*'s inflated circulation of 1,500.

The unimpressive town—known as Mudtown, Stumptown, or The Clearing—had a vital civic life and a booming economy. Two steam lumber mills, two flour mills, two busy wharves, and several active lumber camps provided lots of jobs. The river was crowded with ships as San Francisco took all the lumber and flour it could get at high prices. There were two churches, two newspapers, a Masonic Lodge, and the Portland Academy and Female Seminary. City government was about a year old. The city council usually met in its members' offices, but the city jail was open for business.

The Oro Fino, the business Lappeus built in Portland, is often called a saloon, but it was far more than that. Lappeus added a theater in 1866, and when it burned down in 1878, it was the largest public hall in the city and included at least three taverns and several shops, besides the swanky Gem Saloon, next door. When the Oro Fino (Spanish for "pure gold") opened its doors, there were at least eight saloons in competition, with more opening all the time. Lappeus did not want just any saloon, he wanted the best saloon in town, so that was what he built—a large, impressive place that everyone knew was the best Portland had to offer.

Jesse Applegate, one of the earliest pioneers in southern Oregon, said the nomads who settled the territory had "no sort of use for towns except to raise hell in them." Raising hell was an important pastime for the bored pioneers and lonely transient workers who populated Oregon in the early days. Days of grinding hard work alternated with long nights of general boredom and little entertainment other than what they could make for themselves. The Gold Rush, spreading from California into southern Oregon and eventually into Washington and Idaho, brought a large infusion of wealth into a cash-strapped region. Prospectors who hit it big, or small, ended up in Portland with bags of gold dust, forcing prices up for everything and creating a voracious market for entertainment.

From the beginning, Portland has taken its role of providing regional entertainment seriously. In 1852, Portland had a subscription library, which would eventually become what Stewart Holbrook called the "best library in the West." The eight saloons in town provided not only drinks and female companionship, but illicit card and dice games (Portland outlawed gambling in 1851, but the law was rarely enforced) as well as a billiard table and bowling alley. Traveling shows, such as O. W. Groom's Bullfight, which was not allowed to perform, and A. V. Caldwell's Circus, which was allowed, came to Portland. We do not know for sure when in 1852 Jim and Chloe Lappeus arrived, but they were probably here by mid-September when the Caldwell Circus performed with Jim's old friend Eduoard Chambreau selling tickets and guarding the cashbox.

Portland did not look like much of a city when Jim and Chloe Lappeus arrived in 1852. (*Portland Police Historical Society*)

After 1866, Lappeus' saloon provided a stage for political meetings and touring theater companies as well as musicians. It also offered Portland's first "variety theater," which featured pretty chorus girls available for "personal" entertainment in private boxes or upstairs rooms. The multiple saloons and taverns inside the growing structure soon had a reputation for high-stakes gambling and Lappeus was publicly called a "blackleg," meaning he was a crooked gambler who regularly cheated.

Rumors continued to dog Lappeus, but they were often spread by envious political opponents, whose motives made their accusations sometimes questionable. Lappeus ignored his opponents' charges and befriended powerful Democrats, like W. S. Ladd, who shared his politics and were able and willing to protect him. Ladd and Josiah Failing led the "Businessmen's Clique," which controlled the local Democratic Party. Their opposition was the moribund Whig Party, led by T. J. Dyer of *The Oregonian*, and the infant Republican Party, under the leadership of Philip Marquam. The Businessmen's Clique gained power in 1853, when Josiah Failing was elected mayor. Their ambitious, bumbling plans shaped Portland in important ways, from cemeteries and parks to the way the river was used for industry.

Jim Lappeus, an early advocate for a permanent police force, shaped law enforcement in the city. He was elected city marshal twice (1859–1861 and 1868–1869) and served twice as chief of the metropolitan police (1870–1877 and 1879–1883), becoming Portland's first career law enforcement officer. Lappeus was generally liked as both marshal and police chief. He established a stable police force and helped give Portland the reputation of a peaceful, civilized city where "law and order" was valued. He set the pattern for law enforcement in Portland that still exists in the twenty-first century, including the use of the police for political ends, a reputation for corruption and "selective" enforcement of laws, and impunity in matters of violence. Lappeus left a permanent mark on Portland when he named a neighborhood "Goose Hollow," a nickname given in frustration at the number of violent confrontations among the rowdy "goose ranchers" that resulted in repeated calls for the marshal to settle disputes.

Two incidents illustrate the general violence of Lappeus' temper. The first occurred in the Bank Exchange Saloon, a "two-bit saloon" (contemporary slang for an upscale joint). On the night of January 11, 1864, James Dodson, a faro dealer, broke the bank at the Oro Fino. The next morning, Lappeus confronted Dodson where he worked, at the Bank Exchange. During the argument, Lappeus attacked Dodson with a Bowie knife and cut his pants-leg open. In defense, Dodson fired a pistol at the ex-marshal, slightly wounding him in the thigh. Dodson was charged with attempted murder but was later only convicted of discharging a firearm in city limits.

The second incident occurred in Salem in January 1872. It gained public notoriety because of the status of the participants. Portland Police Chief Lappeus dined with James D. Fay, president of the state senate and a fellow Democrat, at Pete's Chop House. As they emerged onto State Street afterward, they met Eugene Semple, editor of the Portland paper *Oregon Herald* and an active Democrat, newly appointed state printer. No one thought to record the point of dispute, so no one knows exactly what they argued about, but Lappeus punched Semple and knocked him to the ground. When Semple recovered his feet, he ran into a nearby saloon, followed by Lappeus and Fay, "who were aiming blows at him all the time." The saloon, "Vic's," belonged to ex-senator and Indian-fighter Victor Tevitt, another active Democrat and old friend of Lappeus. Semple drew his pistol and cut "deep gashes" on Lappeus' head with the butt of the gun, before then throttling and beating Fay. Tevitt intervened with a "loaded cane" and Lappeus and Fay joined in with their canes, before Semple finally fled. It is clear that when violence occurred, it was often "The Chief" who both started and ended it.

Both Lappeus' breaks in service, as marshal and chief, were caused by scandals. The very first case he worked on as marshal was surrounded by the same rumors about his conduct as those surrounding his last case, the Brown Murder, which would bring his career to an end in 1883. The first case Jim Lappeus handled as marshal, when he took office in 1859, was the notorious Balch case. Danforth Balch, a homesteader with a valuable land claim, shot and killed his son-in-law Mortimer Stump in November 1858, angered that Stump had married Balch's daughter without his consent. Balch was tried for murder and sentenced to death, but easily escaped from the falling-down city jail still being used while the new jail was under construction. In April 1859, Lappeus was elected to replace Marshal Samuel Holcomb. His first order of business was to execute Danforth Balch.

Balch was easy to find, of course, as he was camping out on his own land, in what would in time become Forest Park. The new jail was built, and it would not be an easy one to escape from. Lappeus brought Balch in and began construction of a gallows outside the city jail on Alder Street. Lappeus never denied the rumors that he offered to "leave the door open" for a payment of $1,000 and he brazenly ignored the charges made against him. Mary Jane Balch, Danforth's wife, who was left with huge real estate holdings and eight young children to support, tried to raise the money, but the deal never paid off. Danforth Balch became the first man executed by Multnomah County with Jim Lappeus as executioner.

The marshal worked alone, a one-man force. His main job was keeping order in the saloons and in the wild streets of the North End, which would later become Old Town. One neighborhood that would be a source of trouble throughout Lappeus' career was the downtown Tenderloin, a block of brothels and prostitute cribs, surrounded by saloons on S.W. Yamhill Street. During Lappeus' first term as marshal, it was the home of Annie Lambert's Deadfall Saloon, a notorious dive that would be the crime scene in the 1866 murder of John Williams. After the Williams murder, the neighborhood acquired the name the "Court of Death" and would be the site of three more notorious murders: James Brown (1881), Emma Merlotin (1885), and Thomas Kenealy (1886). Several other mysterious deaths occurred there that remained unsolved. It may also have been the home of Mary J. Sullivan, a young Irish woman recently arrived in Portland, who made her living with laundry and prostitution.

When Lappeus regained the Marshal's office in 1868, he supervised a small force of deputies, but in 1860, he had the authority to swear-in help only in certain circumstances, such as on Election Day. It was the actions of special deputies on Election Day 1860 that led to Lappeus being defeated in the election of April 1861. Lappeus was accused of keeping non-Democrat voters away from the polls and tampering with the ballots in a scandal that became known as the "Oro Fino Ring."

Public indignation over the perceived use of special deputies to suppress the Republican vote added to the smoldering rumors that "the Chief" could be bribed. This resulted in William Grooms' election to his second term as city marshal (his first was 1853–54). Lappeus remained a private citizen until 1868. The time that he was out of

The Oro Fino Theater and Gem Saloon provided the city's largest gathering place and most luxurious dinking and gambling. (*Portland Police Historical Society*)

office saw a great deal of change in Portland. The Civil War caused the city to see a significant rise in violence, and the marshal was authorized to hire two regular deputies. Lappeus was involved in the Bank Exchange shooting in 1864 and expanded the Oro Fino in 1866. The addition of a theater stage to Lappeus' saloon created an important venue for public and political meetings, but it still had a reputation for criminality and violence. In 1867, Thomas G. O'Connor, one of the marshal's deputies, died after a shooting on the sidewalk in front of the Oro Fino, located on First Avenue between Oak and Stark.

Lappeus continued to be an active Democrat, but the party was torn over the issue of slavery. Lappeus, who opposed slavery, worked closely with the progressive wing of the Republican Party, in the newly formed Union Party. The hot disputes within the Democratic Party often resulted in strong personal animosity and sometimes in violence, as we see in the case of the fight in 1872 with Eugene Semple. The "Copperhead" Democrats, who supported the Confederacy's succession and some of whom advocated independence for a new Pacific Republic, were soon driven from the party and Lappeus, with his powerful friends behind him, was re-elected marshal in 1868.

The 1860s transformed Portland as its population nearly tripled—from 2,800 to 8,200. The official population numbers tell only a small part of the story as the migrant workers and Indians spending the wet season in Portland could temporarily triple the city's population. The mining boom in eastern Washington and Idaho created huge amounts of wealth for some, such as William S. Ladd who opened Portland's first bank, called Ladd and Tilton. It also provided huge numbers of cash-flush workers looking for a good time—men who did back-breaking jobs in isolated locations and were bursting for a chance to cut loose, "raise hell," and have a little fun.

Portland was beginning to have an urban appearance; new brick buildings, like Ladd's bank, gave the city a look of permanence and refined elegance. Portland's more than 100 saloons, from Lambert's Deadfall Saloon in the Tenderloin to the new Gem Saloon at the Oro Fino, were ready to take the visitors' cash and let them "raise hell" within limits. The marshal's job was to enforce those limits. Lappeus, a proud saloon owner, understood the importance of the liquor trade; it provided more than two-thirds of the city's tax revenue. As a "blackleg" gambler, Lappeus did not believe in giving a sucker an even break, and as a businessman, he was always open to opportunity, even if it meant deceiving someone or profiting from their inexperience.

The marshal received no salary. He was paid on a piece-rate/per job basis. Jim Lappeus, during both terms as marshal, was the highest-paid marshal on record. The pay-for-service tradition endured in the Portland police for decades as officers gained a reputation for being open to financial opportunity. Eduoard Chambreau, Lappeus' old friend, who kept a saloon in Portland from time to time, describes a "badger game" (in which an unwitting victim was manipulated into paying a large sum of money). This scam involved the cop on the beat, who shared some of the proceeds. Another tradition Lappeus introduced into Portland policing was the selective enforcement of prostitution laws and the profit he received from that business.

Prostitution was of course big business. Many saloons, like the Oro Fino, had rooms upstairs for their "entertainers," but the ones that did not were convenient to the *bagnios* along Yamhill Street between Second and Third. Large wooden boarding houses flanked the now-departed Deadfall Saloon; these resorts featured musical entertainment and companionship under the watchful leadership of independent businesswomen, like the colorful Carrie Bradley (whom we will learn about in the next chapter). Behind the buildings on Yamhill, a collection of one-room "cribs" filled the block toward Taylor Street, and they were bustling with activity.

Marshal Lappeus was a believer in containment, one of the oldest theories of law enforcement, in which certain crimes are tolerated within limits. It has always been the prevailing theory in Portland. The rough crowd raised hell in the bloody, brawling North End. Those with taste found a more refined and alluring hell in the Tenderloin. The city got its cut in the fines it charged for various crimes punished by the Police Court. Jim Lappeus got his cut in more private and questionable transactions.

Portland State University professor Charles Tracy, the first historian to consider the formation of the Portland police and their role in the city, has said that a police force is a quasi-military protective force. The question that must be settled is: what and whom do the police protect? James Lappeus' answer to this question was his most lasting legacy. Under Lappeus and his successors, it was clear that the Portland police protected the wealthy class, especially the downtown merchants and those who dealt in vice, often while maintaining the image of respectable and dedicated family men.

Another legacy Lappeus left with the Portland police had to do with the violence of his volatile nature and the ability of the city to hold the police accountable. Lappeus was involved in several violent acts during his career in and out of the police force. Although the city government investigated Lappeus for malfeasance on several occasions and fired him for cause twice, it never seriously considered the violence he perpetrated or held him accountable for it. No starker example of this manner of indifference occurred than the pitiful death of Mary Sullivan in December 1881.

Mary Sullivan was an Irish immigrant who arrived in Portland around 1861 and made her living with a combination of prostitution and laundry work. She arrived in town when Jim Lappeus was in his first term as city marshal and most likely worked in one of the tenderloin *bagnios*. In 1881, she was what *The Oregonian* called an "abandoned woman" (a nineteenth-century euphemism for an ex-prostitute), who was often sick and homeless. What happened to her on the evening of December 8, 1881, when she went to a friend's room above the notorious Beehive Saloon is well recorded in *The Oregonian*. Fearing she might have a contagious disease, her friend gave up his room and locked the sick older woman inside. The saloonkeeper called Chief Lappeus, the city officer responsible for controlling contagion and communicable disease.

In 1881, Lappeus was reaching the end of his long career in the Portland police. In his early fifties, Lappeus had been a heavy drinker for more than thirty years. A veteran of political fighting he had won the latest battle with the Republicans when he was reinstated as chief in 1879. The charges brought against him in 1877, which involved his drinking on duty and did not even hint at the worst of his misdeeds, were seen as purely political and the reinstated chief must have seemed untouchable at that point. Since the 1860s, the marshal and city police had the responsibility to quarantine people with a contagious illness and the chief oversaw the local City Pest House, as it was called,

By the time James Lappeus left office for good in 1883, he had established a stable and effective police force. (*Portland Police Historical Society*)

where they were confined. Lappeus arrived at the Beehive Saloon on that cold night in 1881 to determine whether Mary Sullivan needed to be confined for the protection of the public or not.

What happened in the rough hotel room above the saloon, where Mary Sullivan sought refuge, will never be known for certain. Jim Lappeus, significantly, was the last person to see her alive. Some of the witnesses said they heard unmistakable sounds of a struggle in the room before Lappeus left. The chief returned to the Central Precinct that night and made the prophetic prediction that the old woman would be "dead by morning." She was. Mary Sullivan was found, naked on the floor, her frail body covered with bruises, the next morning. The coroner's jury ruled that she had died from violence, evidenced by the nakedness and severe bruising on her emaciated body. Lappeus dismissed the coroner's findings. He said she had suffered a fit, throwing herself against the wall and causing the extensive bruising before she died. Even in 1881, the chief's story did not hold water, but his authority ruled and Sullivan's death was never investigated, despite direct, and for the time courageous, findings by the coroner who went on the record contradicting Lappeus' claims.

By the time Mary Sullivan's apparent murder was swept under the rug, Jim Lappeus had less than two years left as police chief. His career ended in 1883 during the scandalous Carrie Bradley case, which we will examine in the next chapter; this time, the charges against Lappeus were more substantial, but the political bias of his enemies was clear and many people refused to believe the chief had broken the law. Regardless, Lappeus' police career was over at the age of fifty-five and he would have only eleven more years to live.

In 1894, when the chief died, *The Oregonian* summed up his career: "His administration was eminently satisfactory, and he enjoyed the confidence of the people, and the respect and obedience of his subordinates." History has not always been kind to Jim Lappeus, which is understandable. Historians have either glossed over his crimes and concentrated only on his positive achievements, or in the rush to parade his numerous crimes, and the rumors about him, his detractors have lost sight of the man. Lappeus achieved many important things for the city, not the least one being a stable police force, but the negative precedents he set are still with us, posing a serious threat to the city more than 130 years later—a reputation for corruption and impunity from responsibility for illegal, and even violent, behavior that routinely goes unpunished.

2

A MORE REFINED HELL

The economic and social inferiority of woman is responsible for prostitution.

Emma Goldman

The most notorious woman in nineteenth-century Portland, Carrie Bradley, only lived here for a few years. It was long enough to make a big impact. Born in Michigan between 1845 and 1850, Bradley came to Portland in 1877. There is little record of her before she left employment at Jenny Moore's brothel in February 1879; after that date, there is no avoiding her. In March 1879, she set herself up in a rambling boarding house at the corner of Second and Yamhill and started making regular appearances in court.

Bradley's *bagnio*, a nineteenth-century euphemism for brothel, was in an infamous neighborhood known as the Tenderloin. This neighborhood, called the Court of Death by *The Oregonian*, centered on the block between Yamhill and Taylor, Second and Third Streets.[1] Long before the North End became Portland's most dangerous neighborhood, the Tenderloin held that title.

The Tenderloin as a vice district had its origins in Annie Lambert's Deadfall Saloon, which opened in 1866. Lambert was notorious as the wife of Jim Lambert, the East Portland hotel owner who went to prison for the Rives Robbery in 1866. Lambert's dive quickly became infamous, not just because it was run by a woman; a lot of rough men hung around there, many of them hoping to get a glimpse of the fortune rumor said Lambert had stashed somewhere. The neighborhood became "the Court of Death" after the 1866 murder of John Williams, which occurred in Lambert's saloon. A decade later, when Lambert was long gone and Bradley moved in, the Tenderloin had the biggest population of prostitutes in the city. In the 1880 census, fifty-eight women listed their occupation as prostitute; almost all of them lived within a block of Carrie Bradley's place.

Bradley's large house dominated the west end of the Tenderloin. The rest of the block, back to Third Street, was filled with one-room "cribs," populated by "French" courtesans. The streets surrounding the prostitution district were lined with saloons, including the notorious Red Light and Mary Cook's Ivy Green. For two decades

Carrie Bradley was the most notorious woman of nineteenth-century Portland. (*Oregon Historical Society*)

The first police headquarters was located at SW 2nd and Oak. The building was replaced in 1912, but it remained police headquarters until the 1980s. (*Portland Police Historical Society*)

(1866–1886), the Court of Death acquired a frightening reputation for violence. Numerous stabbings, a few mysterious disappearances, and at least two cases of Chinese men thrown from upper-story windows occurred there. All of the high-profile murders of the era—from John Williams in 1866 to Thomas Kennealy, whose body was found in the abandoned construction site known as Villiard's Ruins (where the Portland Hotel was later built) in 1886—occurred in the Tenderloin.

The North End, the neighborhood known today as "Old Town," already had a reputation for working-class violence, especially barroom brawls and street riots. The Tenderloin, with upscale hotels like the National close by, served a more discerning clientele in a more refined version of Hell, but the violence was even worse.

The imposing Taylor Street Methodist Church, Portland's first, squatted like a prison matron on the corner of Third and Taylor, across the street from the courtesans' cribs. Twelve years later, as crime took over the neighborhood, the church moved into a new building a block west and changed its name to First Methodist. The congregation included several powerful men including John F. Caples, who was district attorney in the

1880s. The church was active in many progressive causes like temperance and female suffrage. Its members, several of them who lived in the neighborhood, kept a close eye on activities in the Tenderloin. The church fought a decades-long battle to clean up the neighborhood, with limited success.

In Portland in the 1880s, although not respectable, prostitution did not have the moral stigma it does today. With opportunities for women severely limited, prostitution was the most lucrative profession for an independent woman. Some prostitutes were well-known and popular, such as Emma Merlotin, murdered in the Court of Death in 1885, and Alice Oberle, memorialized in the 1890s in Lone Fir Cemetery by a beautiful Celtic cross erected (according to legend) by her grateful clients. Carrie Bradley gained a level of fame, but her personality made her very hard to like.

Portland outlawed prostitution in the 1850s, but the selectively enforced laws and low fines amounted to little more than cutting the city in on a profitable enterprise. In accordance with the law enforcement theory of containment, prostitution was allowed in certain areas within specific limits. Most prostitutes, protected by wealthy or powerful men who took the lion's share of their earnings, had little to fear from the law. Carrie Bradley preferred young, less intelligent men she could easily dominate. Fiercely independent and flaunting the elegance of her house, Bradley faced a form of legal harassment—appearing in court more than a dozen times in six years.

Bradley liked men, but they never seemed to be very good to her. She married George Gill in Michigan in 1873, and although there is no record of divorce or widowhood, in 1880, she claimed to be married to "Harry Bradley." Bradley, of course, was her maiden name and Harry turned out to be a twenty-two-year-old Norwegian immigrant named Harry Peterson who became a petty thief and an alcoholic derelict. There is little chance they were legally married, but *The Oregonian* called him her husband as it reported the escalating charges of domestic violence and prostitution that broke up the "marriage" before the end of the year.

Her next lover, Charley Hamilton, was even more dangerous. Hamilton was a well-known thug with a long record of violent crime and a large cast of hoodlum friends. Bradley had him arrested twice—once for robbing her and the second time for assaulting her, setting fire to her place, and burning her badly. Although Hamilton was violent to her on several occasions, there must have been sympathy between them. He gave her a pair of brass knuckles made to fit her hand, and when she needed to get rid of a body, Charley was the one she called.

Another man who became important to Carrie Bradley was Pete Sullivan. Born in Ireland, Sullivan came to San Francisco with his family when he was three years old, in 1860. He was sick when he came to Portland in early 1881 and hooked up with Mollie Flippen, a young woman from a prosperous Hillsboro family who worked for Bradley. Bradley immediately liked the young man and invited him to move into her house. She paid for a doctor to fix him up. She taught him to recruit young girls for her brothel. Soon, he was also sharing Carrie's bed.

The events surrounding the death of James Nelson Brown in October 1881 have been told many times, but the truth is elusive.[2] The story told by one of the participants in the murder, Dolly Adams, has been accepted as the true story for more than 125 years, but no one had more reason to lie about what happened than Dolly Adams. She would never even tell the truth about her real name. Her story, obviously skewed to support her own innocence, put the blame for the killing squarely on Carrie Bradley.

Above: In the 1880s, police officers patrolled on foot with assistance from a horse-drawn paddy wagon. (*Portland Police Historical Society*)

Left: Pete Sullivan, an Irish immigrant, was a central figure in Carrie Bradley's murder trial. After their release from prison, Sullivan and Bradley moved to California together. (*Folsom Prison Archive*)

Bradley told a slightly different story, backed up by Pete Sullivan, blaming Adams for the murder and claiming that Bradley only helped hide the body after the killing. The other girls who worked in Bradley's house backed up Adams' story, saying they saw Bradley dose Brown's drinks with morphine and wipe his face with a handkerchief soaked in chloroform before having him put to bed upstairs. In Adams' story, Bradley wanted Brown dead so he would not be able to testify against her. In addition, hard-hearted Bradley beat the corpse with her brass knuckles, taking out her frustrations on the dead man. The coroner found that the body was badly beaten after death, adding weight to Dolly's testimony.

It was probably not a coincidence that James Brown died the night before he was scheduled to testify against Adams and Bradley on robbery charges. Brown, a retired timber-spotter from southwest Washington, arrived in Portland a week or two before his death with a great deal of cash—by some reports, over $4,000 ($98,000 today). Brown spent his time in Portland gambling, drinking, and visiting brothels in what seemed to be a mad dash to spend his fortune, but the chances that he went through that much money so fast are slim. For a man intent on spending a great deal of money, it is unusual that Dolly Adams' theft of $6 from his pocket should be so important, but it was the principle that bothered Brown. He swore that he would prosecute Adams and Bradley to the full extent of the law.

Brown's accusations came at a bad time for Carrie Bradley, who was facing four indictments for running a "house of ill repute." District Attorney John Caples made it an important goal of his terms as D.A. to clean out the open vice district in the Tenderloin. Caples agreed with Police Chief Lappeus' "containment" plan, but he wanted vice contained in the North End, where he owned property and could profit from illegal activity and not in the neighborhood just across the street from the politically powerful Taylor Street Church. Caples targeted Carrie Bradley because of her independence and flaunting the law; he worked for more than a year to get the indictments against her. Several men had been drugged and/or robbed at Bradley's, but none of them would come forward to testify, fearing the effect it would have on their reputations. When Brown agreed to testify about being robbed, Caples saw his chance to put Bradley out of business once and for all.

Bradley apparently thought Caples had power over her, too. According to Dolly Adams' story, Bradley was relentless in her pursuit of Brown, urging Pete Sullivan to track him down and get him back to her house. When Sullivan finally did get Brown alone, Bradley herself persuaded the reluctant man to come back to her *bagnio*, where she was methodical as she killed him in cold blood. Bradley's depiction of herself as a golden-hearted angel, who tried to convince mean Mr. Brown not to prosecute, and then, only after being confronted with his murder, helped to dispose of an inconvenient corpse, is far less believable than the story of proven liar Dolly Adams.

Bradley's trial for murder was treated as entertainment by many in Portland. The courtroom was jammed with spectators every day of the trial and *The Oregonian* reported on Bradley's fashionable clothes and cold attitude as if she were the star of the show. The trial was full of irregularities that in the twentieth century would have resulted in a mistrial. For example, the main witness for the prosecution, Dolly Adams, refused to reveal her true identity, but was allowed to testify anyway; also, just as District Attorney Caples finished his closing statement, Sam Simmons, a policeman who

The City Jail, although it had no facilities for women, was Carrie Bradley's home for more than a year as she participated in the various trials and investigations surrounding her case. (*Portland Police Historical Society*)

had been a witness for the prosecution, stepped forward and arrested two of the defense attorneys on charges of attempting to bribe jurors. Neither attorney was convicted of a crime, but the jury could not help but be influenced by the arrest. The jury did not take long to convict Bradley of manslaughter; she was sentenced to twelve years. Sullivan pled guilty and received a five-year sentence.

After Brown's disappearance, still weeks before his body was discovered, Bradley pled guilty to one of the charges against her. She paid a fine of $100 and the other charges were dropped. Brown's death, over a petty theft, seemed pointless until you consider that Brown had several thousand dollars at the time of his death, and no one seems to have asked what happened to it. About a year after being convicted of manslaughter, Carrie Bradley was the main witness against Police Chief Lappeus in the bribery investigation that ended his career. Several witnesses came forward to say that Bradley was deep in debt and could not possibly have raised the $1,000 she said she paid the chief to allow her to leave town. In debt she may have been, but in February 1882, when the murder case was coming to a head, Bradley, Charley Hamilton, Pete Sullivan, and several other of the accomplices left town, spending large amounts of money on

Sam Simmons (seated third from right) was one of Portland's first high-profile police officers. Although he never achieved his ambition to become chief, he was involved in many important cases in the 1880s and 1890s. (*Portland Police Historical Society*)

steamship tickets and hotels in Victoria, B.C., and San Francisco. Money did not seem to be a problem.

The bribery case against Police Chief James Lappeus is probably Bradley's largest legacy to Portland because it brought an end to Lappeus' long career. Charges against Lappeus arose about a year after Bradley was sentenced. In May 1883, Rev. E. F. Heroy, a lay minister and member of the Taylor Street Methodist Church, and Dr. Mary A. Thompson, one of the first female doctors in the state and an active member of the First Unitarian Church, accused Chief Lappeus of making an alliance with saloon and brothel owners in the Tenderloin.

Specific charges against the chief accused him of accepting a bribe of $1,000 from Carrie Bradley to allow her and accomplices to escape the city while under investigation for murder; allowing the Red Light Saloon and the Ivy Green, as well as the proprietors of several brothels, to sell liquor without a license; allowing saloon owner Adam Zorn to sell liquor to underage girls; and allowing the prostitutes in the Tenderloin to openly solicit customers from the windows and doors of their establishments.

Mayor James Chapman immediately suspended Chief Lappeus and tried to replace him, but the City Council stopped his actions, forming a committee to investigate the charges. The investigation lasted several weeks, and many interesting points came out in testimony. Some of the witnesses admitted that they were coached by Sam Simmons, who was actively trying to get Lappeus' job for himself. Simmons attended every day of the investigation and openly advised the prosecuting attorney while examining the witnesses. District Attorney Caples claimed that Lappeus had done everything possible to bring Bradley and her accomplices to justice, but his timetable of the case is suspicious and it appears Lappeus, although he suspected Bradley was the killer, did not approach Caples with his information until after she had left town. In addition, Caples called the verdict against Bradley into question when he admitted that Dolly Adams and Molly Flippen, his two strongest witnesses against her, could not be relied on to tell the truth, even under oath.

The Oregonian's coverage of the investigation was openly partisan even though the paper declared itself neutral in the case. The paper's coverage slandered witnesses and attorneys and declared the investigation a waste of time, indicating through its language that the reader should ignore the whole thing. The coverage of one of the late days of the investigation on which several important witnesses gave testimony, including Lappeus himself, ran under the headline "Terribly Tedious." On the last day of testimony, the headline refers to the "alleged investigation." There is an unexplained gap in reporting on the day the committee traveled to Salem to interview Carrie Bradley herself, and there does not seem to be any existing record of what she had to say, although *The Oregonian* reported extensively on hearsay evidence that she claimed she had been promised an early pardon if Lappeus was removed from office.

On June 20, 1883, the Justice Committee reported to the City Council that all of the charges against Lappeus were "entirely groundless and without foundation." On the editorial page, *The Oregonian* said the charges were brought against the chief by "a political ring of unsavory reputation." The editorial crowed, "Lappeus has been strengthened in his position and will pretty certainly stay in it." Lappeus denied all the charges against him and then was exonerated by the investigating committee, but ironically, he was replaced as police chief less than a month later. *The Oregonian* virtually ignored the change.[3]

The long reign of James Lappeus, Portland's first career law enforcement officer, was over. Carrie Bradley's short, unhappy career was on hold while she cooled her heels, along with Pete Sullivan, in the state penitentiary in Salem. Whether or not Bradley was promised an early pardon if Lappeus lost his job, she was pardoned in 1886 after serving about three years of her twelve-year sentence for manslaughter. Pete Sullivan was released around the same time and the two of them set up a new brothel in Sisson (now Mount Shasta), California. It all came to light in 1894 when Sullivan was arrested in San Francisco for the abduction of two young women who ended up working in Bradley's new house. Sullivan spent the next five years in San Quentin. In 1896, Bradley shot herself, ending a life that could not have been very happy.

3

MONEY TALKS

You men corrupt all you touch.

Francis Heney

Self-government was one of the main motives for pioneers to come to Oregon in the nineteenth century; it has never been smooth or easy. The process of learning to govern the city of Portland has been trial and error, characterized by periods of radical experimentation alternating with entrenched reaction. Most of the people involved in governing Portland believed and acted as if their personal interests and those of the city were the same. Many of them enriched themselves at public expense, though probably none as extensively as John H. Mitchell.

Born John Mitchell Hipple in Butler County, Pennsylvania, in 1835, Mitchell was a man that women found attractive. Blessed with luxurious brown hair, soft blue eyes, and an attractive smile, Mitchell's looks were disarming. Polished rhetorical skills, usually in a demagogic style, combined with personal charm, made him nearly unstoppable as a politician. Mitchell was a man who provoked strong reactions from others. People either loved him or hated him, often one after the other. Historian Kimbark Macoll said, "No one in Oregon's history has ever aroused more popular enthusiasm or more intense animosity."

Mitchell started out as a schoolteacher, but the ethical lapses that characterized his life ended his teaching career when he seduced his fifteen-year-old student, Sadie Hoon. A child, Jessie, was born, and the teacher married the student. The couple had two more children in quick succession, but their marriage was not a happy one. Soon, Mitchell moved another schoolteacher, a woman named Maria J. Brinker, into his house where they carried on an open sexual affair. Sadie complained about the unusual relationship, and her husband threatened to kill her if she ever brought the subject up again.

By 1860, Mitchell had turned his hand to law and was partner in a law firm, but his domestic situation had become unsupportable. In April, Mitchell left Pennsylvania with his oldest daughter and his adulterous lover, Maria. For capital, he "borrowed" $4,000 from his law partner, who did not see him again for several years. Mitchell and Brinker

John H. Mitchell in his senatorial office, 1899. Kimbark Macoll said, "No one in Oregon's history has ever aroused more popular enthusiasm or more intense animosity." (*Oregon Historical Society*)

Over the course of his career, the municipal judges of Portland's police court became important cogs in Mitchell's political machine. (*Oregon Historical Society*)

went to San Luis Obispo, California, where he opened a law office and introduced his lover as his wife. Only a couple of months passed before Mitchell and his daughter came north to Portland without Maria Brinker. He now called himself John H. Mitchell.

Although he was never accepted by Portland's establishment, Mitchell soon created a place for himself in the new community, being appointed city attorney. His law practice specialized in probate cases, and he made a habit of acquiring the property of his clients at bargain-basement prices. He was later accused of stealing large portions of the Balch homestead (the land grant of Danforth Balch, the first man executed for murder by Multnomah County) from the man's heirs, leaving them in poverty. In a characteristic move, when the Balch children came of age and sued him, Mitchell defended himself by invoking the statute of limitations, which had expired, leaving him untouchable. In the Caruthers case, another probate involving an early Portland settler's estate, Mitchell apparently brought in a phony heir under an assumed name and ended up the owner of another valuable piece of property, this time south of Portland. By 1870, the young lawyer had amassed a fortune worth $50,000 ($855,000 today).

In 1862, Mitchell formed a law partnership with Joseph Dolph, another recently arrived attorney, and together, they created a law firm that became one of the most powerful in the state. Dolph and Mitchell's partnership did not survive the political battles of the 1870s, but over the next four decades, three members of the firm, including Mitchell himself, were elected to the U.S. Senate. The basis for much of their power came from the relationship Dolph and Mitchell developed with railroad speculator Ben Holladay, another businessman hated by the Portland establishment. Holladay, fresh from the sale of his California–Utah stagecoach line to Wells Fargo and flush with cash, became interested in Portland in the 1860s. In 1868, Holladay made Portland his headquarters and hired Mitchell as his personal attorney.

Holladay was never shy about throwing around his wealth to further his ends. At one point, he bragged about spending $35,000 in the state legislature to secure the old Central Oregon Railroad land grants for his new railroad corporation, the Oregon and California, known as the O&C. Politically ambitious, Mitchell served two terms in the state senate starting in 1862 and was elected senate president in 1864. Although his plan to be elected U.S. senator failed in 1866, he continued to work toward that goal and accumulated wealth by handling Holladay's convoluted affairs. In 1867, finally able to smooth things over back in Pennsylvania, Mitchell repaid part of the money he had taken from his ex-law partner and bribed his abandoned wife to finally agree to a divorce. The divorce came a little late since he bigamously married another woman, Martha "Mattie" Price, in Portland in 1862.

During Mitchell's first campaign for state senate, as a candidate of the Union Party, he became famous for delivering fiery, hour-long speeches, equating a vote for the Democratic Party with a vote for secessionists and traitors. Mitchell's scorched-earth politics served him well in a political career that lasted more than forty years, but it also left him vulnerable to attacks on his character and created bitter, life-long enemies such as industrialist Henry W. Corbett and Joseph Simon, a law clerk and later partner of Dolph and Mitchell. In the days when the U.S. senator was appointed by the state legislature, Mitchell was a candidate for the office at least eight times. He was elected four times and served over twenty years in the U.S. Senate.

Some historians have called the Portland election of 1872 the city's most corrupt, but it was only the beginning. The tactics used by what *The Oregonian* was soon calling the Holladay-Mitchell Ring set the tone for dirty elections for generations to come. Many years later, Ned Wicks, the owner of the American Exchange Saloon at the time, reminisced about Holladay handing him a bag of $2.50 gold coins that Wicks used to hire repeat voters in heavily Democratic districts. Ben Holladay bragged to Judge Matthew Deady about spending $20,000 to make Oregon a Republican state. As part of the bargain, Holladay helped elect three city council members and made his personal attorney a U.S. senator. Whatever the cause, Republican turnout was heavy in Multnomah County and Democrats were surprised by Republican strength in districts they had formerly counted on. John Mitchell, who was widely quoted saying, "Ben Holladay's politics are my politics and what Ben Holladay wants is what I want," was elected to the U.S. Senate, but he was only getting started.

Mitchell had a talent for turning allies into enemies. No enemy was more bitter against Mitchell than his old ally from the Union Party, Henry W. Corbett. An original Portland merchant settler, Corbett arrived in Portland in early 1851 only one month after the city was chartered. His nearest rival for wealth, William S. Ladd, arrived four months after Corbett, and the two men became lifelong friends and collaborators. Where Ladd was a Democrat, Corbett had been a Whig and was an enthusiastic supporter of the Republican Party when it began in 1854. Corbett's business achievements are far too numerous to list here, but he was known for dominating the hardware market. He had his hand in virtually every aspect of the development of Portland, from rope-making to street-paving to the Willamette Ironworks, which created Portland's characteristic cast-iron building ornaments. It could be argued that Corbett was the most important industrialist of nineteenth-century Portland. In addition, Henry Corbett was a lifelong Republican activist and kingmaker who wielded a great deal of personal and professional power.

Corbett was adept at finding common cause with Portland's Democratic majority and forging political coalitions. The Union Party, bringing "War Democrats" together with progressive Republicans during the Civil War, was one of Corbett's many achievements, and it propelled him to the U.S. Senate in 1866, despite an unexpected challenge from Oregon Senate President John Mitchell. Six years later, Corbett was defeated in his attempt to return to Washington by the upstart Mitchell.

From the time Corbett took office in 1867, he began to flex his financial muscles. He established Portland's First National Bank, which was backed by U.S. treasury bonds and able to issue federal currency, in 1869. He also built two downtown buildings during his time in the Senate—The Corbett Building on First between Alder and Washington

Union Depot as seen from the Steel Bridge, Portland, Ore. 027
Portland Archives, A2004-002.646

John Mitchell was sometimes referred to as a "creature of the railroads." He spent much of his career protecting the interests of Ben Holliday and Jay Gould. (*Portland City Archive*)

and The Corbett Block (not completed until 1874) located on Front and Alder. It was no surprise when he bought *The Oregonian* in 1872, shortly after it became clear he would not be going back to Washington.

Corbett wasted no time when he took control of *The Oregonian*. He fired Harvey W. Scott, who supported Mitchell a little too openly in the recent election, and replaced him as editor with City Councilman William Lair Hill, who began running long columns exposing the past life of John Hipple Mitchell, "the Senator with two lives." Mitchell dealt with the embarrassing allegations the way he always did—first denying them, then admitting them, but downplaying their importance. Mitchell openly appealed for sympathy, implying that everyone had embarrassing things in their past and he was no different. The Senate Ethics Committee ruled that they had no jurisdiction over bad acts that senators committed before being elected and Mitchell took his seat in Congress.

Ben Holladay, in his quest to control the railroads in Oregon, overextended himself, and Mitchell's first term as senator coincided with Holladay's long, steady financial decline. In Washington D.C., Mitchell found fertile ground for his corrupt schemes and soon was receiving payoffs from Jay Gould, the railroad tycoon whose manipulations helped create financial panics in 1869 and again in 1873. The main "achievement' of Mitchell's first term in the Senate was delaying the westward expansion of the Northern Pacific railroad, which benefited both of his railroad tycoon sponsors: Holladay, whose O&C Railroad depended on the fact that there was no other railroad connection to Portland, and, Gould, whose Union Pacific Railroad enjoyed a monopoly on transcontinental shipping. Mitchell's machinations resulted in a decade-long delay in bringing a transcontinental railroad to Portland.

The other major "achievement" of Mitchell's first term in the Senate was covering up the mess made by the Multnomah County election of 1872. Election irregularities in Portland were obvious and two federal grand juries were empaneled to investigate and prosecute violations of the law. The first grand jury was dismissed amid allegations of jury tampering. The second grand jury was stopped when Mitchell pressured his old Union Party colleague George H. Williams, who had been appointed attorney general by President Grant in 1871, to fire U.S. attorney for Oregon A. C. Gibbs, a former Oregon governor. Williams, whom historian Malcolm Clark called a "weak man," had been nominated as chief justice of the Supreme Court early in 1873 and needed Mitchell's support in the Senate. Bowing to pressure from Senator Mitchell, he fired Gibbs, ending the investigation of the 1872 election. A few months later, under fire for alleged bribery and other financial scandals, Williams' nomination was withdrawn, and he resigned from the Justice Department a few months later.

The "Gibbs Affair" was just one of a long series of scandals that rocked the Grant Administration, but it secured Mitchell's seat in the Senate once and for all. Not much is known about Mitchell's participation in the corrupt presidential election of 1876, in which Republican Rutherford B. Hayes snatched the presidency away from the popular vote winner, Democrat Samuel Tilden, but Mitchell was a strong Hayes supporter and a disputed Oregon electoral vote was central to the Republican victory. It is outside the scope of this book, but that could be a profitable subject for future research.

Mitchell confidently started his campaign for re-election in 1878 with the slogan "No one has done more for Oregon than Senator Mitchell," but *The Oregonian* was not alone in being unable to identify what he had actually accomplished that was good for the state. Opposition to Mitchell and his brand of politics coalesced in the formation of a "Citizens' Ticket" that put Henry Failing, Corbett's closest ally, into City Hall. With Corbett's strength consolidated in Multnomah County, Mitchell's only hope for re-election was cold cash, but Ben Holladay, broke and beset by personal problems, was not there to back him up. Democrat James Slater was elected to the Senate. It might have been the first time that personal opposition to John Mitchell split the Republican Party, allowing a Democratic victory. It certainly would not be the last.

Mitchell, who was comfortable in his role of "creature of the corporations," remained in Washington D.C. as a lobbyist, although he returned regularly to Portland and continued to practice law. Mitchell was a pioneer in direct mail marketing of legal services with his campaign to identify Civil War soldiers eligible for government pensions in 1882. Mitchell had not given up his political ambitions, and he vied to be U.S. senator again in 1882, but this time, he had a strong opponent in Joseph "Little Joe" Simon, who had consolidated power for the Republican Party in Oregon in 1880 and was a junior law partner of Joseph Dolph. He opposed Mitchell, who eventually endorsed his ex-law partner. Joseph Dolph was elected to the Senate, and Mitchell continued to build his power in the dominant political party. By 1885, he was strong enough to be returned to the Senate where he stayed until the debacle of 1897.

Simon had supported Mitchell in 1872, but the two men became bitter enemies, and Portland politics of the 1880s and 1890s is characterized by a battle between Simon with his urban political machine and Mitchell with rural support and crossover Democratic votes. Simon had another strong ally in the fight—a man who had also supported Mitchell and then turned against him: Harvey W. Scott.

Scott took over the editorship of Ben Holladay's newspaper, the *Portland Daily Bulletin*, during the 1873 election, but soon went broke along with the railroad tycoon. Amusingly, Henry Corbett sold *The Oregonian* back to Henry Pittock in 1877 and Scott returned as the editor. In 1882, Mitchell and Scott fought an open war of words in the pages of *The Oregonian*. Scott, who had an elegant genius for writing, accused the ex-senator of "flatulent oratory" and exposed the dirty dealings of the Balch and Carruthers probate cases. Scott's revelations were instrumental in Mitchell's withdrawal from the race for the Senate in 1882, but the men may have come to some kind of arrangement or understanding. After the election of 1882, *The Oregonian*'s coverage of Mitchell dried up. The re-elected senator was rarely mentioned, and hardly ever in a negative light.

Mitchell spent most of his time on the east coast after 1885. He only made rare appearances at the Portland Hotel, usually just before elections, where he held court like visiting royalty and sent frequent telegrams commenting on local and national issues to influential friends in Oregon. Loyal henchmen, like Charles Carey and Albert Tanner (both of whom served terms as municipal court judges), looked after Mitchell's political interests, but "Little Joe" Simon, backed by Henry Corbett's money, took control of the city government. Mitchell was only able to secure his Senate seat (by one vote) in 1885 by appealing to Democrats for support. Simon, who also controlled the State legislature, had the majority of the Republican Party on his side, but Mitchell was able to beat him down by splitting the party.

The Northern Pacific Railroad finally reached Portland in 1883, while Mitchell was out of office. The railroad changed Portland dramatically and population boomed,

As senator, John Mitchell spent most of his time in Washington D.C. The Portland Hotel was his headquarters on infrequent visits home. (*Portland City Archive*)

nearly tripling between 1880 and 1890. A seemingly endless supply of cheap labor poured into the city, fueling industrial growth and all manner of strife. Portland, hemmed in by the verdant West Hills and the increasingly polluted Willamette River, needed room to expand, but the independent cities of East Portland (founded in 1872) and Albina (founded in 1887) blocked growth to the east. In addition, East Portland, with its rapidly expanding industrial capacity, and Albina, with railyards and a new shipyard, could become economic rivals of the Rose City. The "political machine," modeled on the politics of East Coast cities, which Joe Simon built, gave Portland the advantage it needed, and the two eastside cities were absorbed in 1891.

The 1880s were a time of grinding poverty for those who worked for a living, but great opportunity for anyone who could gather a sum of capital, by any means. Some of the "carpetbaggers" (Yankee veterans who carried their capital in satchels made of carpet), like James Lotan, who came west after the Civil War, prospered. Remittance-men (who received a regular allowance to stay far away from their respectable East Coast families), like Jonathan Bourne, Jr., found a warm welcome in Portland. Bunco-men (who lived by their wits, greed, and confidence) flourished. Many fortunes were made, and more were lost in the alternate cycle of boom-and-bust that led up to the first "great depression" in 1893, but the power of the suffering working class was growing and their voice would be heard.

The two main political parties began to compete for the growing working-class vote. The Democrats, recovered from the Civil War and under a new generation of leadership, made common cause with the rising Labor movement, but they appealed to the most militant and racist elements in Portland. The Republicans appealed to the ethnic loyalty of working-class voters, creating a kind of identity politics that rewarded the loyalty of ethnic groups with patronage jobs. For example, in the 1890s, Joe Simon won the vote of Portland's African American community with help from black orators, such as Julius Caesar and S. S. Freeman; they were rewarded with Portland's first black city employees.[1] Both of these methods drew working-class voters, but as the economic pain increased, the People's Party (later the Populist Party) began to build strength with radical proposals designed to solve the problem of poverty at its root.

Although Simon lost the battle with Mitchell for the Senate in 1885, his faction did elect the governor. As a result, Simon was appointed to a newly re-organized police commission, with Jonathan Bourne, Jr., another of the board's three members. Bourne, a "remittance man" from Massachusetts, was Portland's most prominent high-living attorney who had come to represent the gambling/saloon interests, and with the help of strongman Larry Sullivan (we will learn more about Sullivan in the next chapter), he came to dominate the politically powerful Second Ward in the North End.

Between them, Simon and Bourne politicized the police force to an extent that would even have shocked ex-Police Chief James Lappeus. Following Lappeus' model, the police hired crowds of "special officers" on Election Day, who had the sole purpose of intimidating undesirable voters and poll watchers. The corruption of the 1872 election, when as many as 25 percent of the votes were questionable, seems quaint compared to the violence, coercion, and open theft of later elections.

Politics in 1890s Portland was dominated by men with little morality, and no loyalties, except to their own self-interest. Joe Simon made frequent appeals to patriotism and American idealism, but his one goal was to dominate the political system as his own personal fiefdom. Jonathan Bourne, a Simon ally who switched to Mitchell in 1896 and then quickly switched back in 1897, was motivated by the "Silver Issue" because he was a major investor in Washington and Idaho mines that produced silver. James Lotan, a carpetbagger who arrived in Portland in 1865, switched back and forth between Simon and Mitchell at whim as he rose rapidly in the Republican Party. Lotan became so untouchable that even an indictment for smuggling opium could not stop his political rise.[2]

Moral flexibility became the most valuable attribute of Portland politicians and businessmen. Lincoln Steffens, the "muckraking" journalist, did not visit Portland until 1905, but he could have been talking about the Rose City when he wrote, "The grafters call for cheers for the flag, 'prosperity' and 'the party,' just as highwaymen command 'hands up.'"

Mitchell managed to stay in the Senate for another term in 1891, but the reaction to the blatant corruption in Portland resulted in a new reform movement that swept the Citizens' Consolidation ticket of new Mayor William S. Mason into office. Simon kept control of the police through the police commission's new chairman, George Frank, who proved as slippery as his other allies. Mayor Mason lamented that the city could not control the police or enforce the laws, and Frank swept into City Hall in another violent election in 1894.

Mayor Mason's attempts to reform the city were scuttled partly by the financial panic of 1893. City revenues dwindled and employees were laid off in all departments.

Unemployment swept the city, and the poverty that the working class knew so well quickly worsened. In 1894, under the leadership of William U'Ren, the Populist Party showed strength at the ballot box and was expected to do much better in the presidential election year of 1896. The issue that would determine the election was the free coinage of silver. Conservatives advocated the "Gold Standard," with the value of the U.S. dollar set by the accrual price of gold. This policy kept money out of circulation in tight economic times. Advocates of "free silver," setting the value of the dollar on the price of gold and silver (at a rate of 16:1), would increase the cash in circulation and relieve some of the pain of the depression, but also inflate prices and lower the value of the dollar.

The issue split the Republican Party so badly they had two candidates for Portland Mayor in 1896—D. Solis Cohen, supported by Simon and Corbett, and Gen. Charles F. Beebee, supported by Mitchell. Jonathan Bourne's candidate, Democratic Governor Sylvester Pennoyer, easily won. Simon's political machine was smashed as Pennoyer used Simon's own tactics against him to destroy what "Little Joe" had built. The city was in turmoil, but John Mitchell came out on top. He arranged a secret deal with Bourne to support him to stay in the Senate. When Mitchell blithely supported the national Republican Party platform, which included support for the Gold Standard, Bourne felt betrayed. The stage was set for the Legislative Hold-Up of 1897.

Bourne swore that John Mitchell would never be elected to the Senate, but he had personally bribed the senators of the coming legislative session and collected their sworn pledges to vote for Mitchell. Bourne knew he had bribed honest men who would stay bought and hit on the only scheme that could stop Mitchell. In a secret agreement with Henry W. Corbett, who provided the cash, and William U'Ren, who picked up and delivered the money from the First National Bank to Bourne's rented quarters in Salem, Bourne created a forty-day party, a veritable state exposition of Portland vice and corruption. Legislators from the distant regions of the state could not pass up the food, drink, and friendly companionship that was available to them in Bourne's apartments. Meanwhile, U'Ren and his delegation of Populist legislators attended every session and employed delaying tactics. A quorum was never reached, and the Senate adjourned without electing a U.S. senator.

The newly elected governor, William Lord, appointed Henry Corbett, but the whole thing stunk so bad the Senate steadfastly refused to seat him, leaving one of Oregon's Senate seats vacant. Now an ex-senator, Mitchell's interests kept him in Washington, and he let Corbett clean up the mess in Portland. William Mason was once again elected mayor in 1898 and began the process of repairing "Little Joe's" machine, before dying suddenly. Simon was elected to the vacant Senate seat that year and found that he was on unfamiliar ground far from home. Mitchell returned to the Senate in 1901. The next year his triumph was complete when Mitchell's old pal, ex-senator, ex-attorney general, ex-supreme court nominee, George H. Williams was elected mayor.

At seventy-nine, George Williams was the oldest person elected to be Portland's mayor so far. He was also the most famous Oregonian of his time, being the first West Coast resident to ever serve in a presidential cabinet. He spent nearly three years as attorney general under President Grant. Williams was a figurehead as the real power in Portland during his term of office was Jack Matthews, who had risen to become John Mitchell's most important deputy. In 1902, Mitchell arranged for Matthews' appointment as an U.S. marshal. Williams' time as mayor unfortunately is not well-remembered. Henry Corbett, who had already proved that self-interest was his most important ideal, said of Williams, "I believe him wholly insincere, except in one thing, that is his own advancement at all hazard." P.S.U. professor Gordon Dodds summed up Mayor Williams: "Behind Williams' distinguished appearance the city lay in the grip of business interests, gamblers and thugs."

Gambling and prostitution, prominent since the founding of the city, had become the pervasive political issue of the day. All of the most respected businesspeople of Portland were implicated in vice crime, often through renting their property to illegal businesses. Sometimes, they were even more directly involved, like Henry Corbett, who had a luxurious gambling club, the Arion, on Southwest Yamhill Street. Williams saw vice as an "unpleasant subject" and preferred to sweep the whole problem under the rug, but popular support for the "anti-vice campaign" would not allow it. The policy of containing vice crime in the North End had the unpleasant side effect of simply making it more visible, especially since it was concentrated around the Union Railroad Depot. Williams, whose main priority was making the city look good for the coming Lewis and Clark Exposition of 1905, encouraged a system of fining gamblers and prostitutes as well as harassing the most indiscreet of these characters to move out of the North End and take their activities elsewhere. Houses of prostitution became an ordinary sight in Irvington and other eastside neighborhoods.

In return for his help in blocking Mitchell's election to the Senate in 1897, William U'Ren extorted support for his Initiative and Referendum Bill, which passed the legislature in 1902. The "direct democracy" system gave the Populist Party the tool they needed to pass the rest of U'Ren's plan, expanding democracy and creating the Oregon System that prevails in most of the country in the twenty-first century. Believing that the problems of Democracy can only be solved by more democracy, U'Ren created the tools to end the "political boss" system that controlled most parts of the country.

John Mitchell began 1904 riding high again. His power in Portland and Washington D.C. seemed unassailable. By the end of the year, all that would suddenly change. On the last day of 1904, President Theodore Roosevelt, at the urging of U.S Attorney Francis Heney, removed Portland's U.S. District Attorney, John H. Hall. He also removed Jack Matthews from his position as U.S. marshal. That same day, Heney's grand jury, which had been investigating fraud in homestead claims in the Cascade Mountains, returned indictments against Senator John Mitchell and Congressman Binger Hermann, for conspiracy and bribery.

The Land Fraud Case was the biggest scandal to hit Portland up to that time, and long overdue. Stephan A. Douglas Puter, a surveyor and speculator who had been involved in similar land fraud since the 1870s, told the story of a particularly complex case in his book *Looters of the Public Domain*. The title of Puter's book is ironic since he personally was one of the biggest looters. In his book, written after receiving a presidential pardon for his crimes, Puter describes a trip he took to Washington D.C. in 1902 to secure deeds to a dozen phony land claims. At the time, Binger Hermann was the commissioner of the General Land Office, and his approval was needed in order to secure the deeds. Hermann insisted on documentation of the phony claims before the deeds could be issued, but Puter was in a hurry and the documentation Hermann demanded was difficult to obtain, since the claims were mostly in the names of people

S. A. D. Puter in his jail cell where he wrote his book *Looters of the Public Domain*, exposing the Land Fraud Scandal of 1905. (*Oregon Historical Society*)

who did not exist. Puter met several times with Senator Mitchell, on one occasion paying the senator with two $1,000 bills for his help in pressuring his fellow Oregonian, Binger Hermann.

Mitchell probably thought nothing of the transaction. He had been dealing with railroad and land grant claims, phony and real, for nearly forty years. He even protested that the bribe was too large and tried to give one of the bills back before he finally accepted. It was the last straw for Mitchell, though. His carefully constructed house of cards began to collapse around him. Hermann was eventually acquitted of wrong-doing, but Mitchell, convicted of bribery and perjury, was sentenced to a year in prison. In the Senate, his enemies began preparing Ethics Committee hearings that could expel the corrupt senator. Seventy-year-old Mitchell returned to Portland after the conviction and died shortly after his arrival back in town. The timing of his death could not have been more fortuitous.

4

BLOOD SPORT, BLOOD MONEY

We lack the power to enforce the laws.

Mayor William S. Mason

Larry Sullivan was a confidence man. With little more than a brazen, boastful nature and powerful muscles, he rose to the very threshold of power before an unexpected collapse brought him to abject poverty and an early death at the age of fifty-five. Born in Massachusetts in 1863, Lawrence Malachi Sullivan grew up in Newport, Rhode Island, before moving as a teenager to Scranton, Pennsylvania, where he worked as a boilermaker and gained a reputation as a violent brawler.

Sullivan came to the Pacific Northwest because the prizefight fad had swept the region in 1885, although boxing was illegal everywhere in the country. David Campbell, a twenty-one-year-old volunteer firefighter destined for greatness, captured Portland's attention with a spectacular knockout during an exhibition of "boxing science" at the Mechanic's Pavilion.[1] At the urging of "Old Joe" Taylor, Portland's first boxing promoter, martial arts "professor" Duncan MacDonald, a retired professional wrestler and showman, came to town and began training "Our Dave" for a highly publicized fight with J. E. "Jumbo" Reilly, a well-known North End bartender and bouncer. The fight was a perfect Victorian morality play with clean-cut, "Adonis-like" Dave Campbell pitted against a grotesque symbol of the North End's culture of vice and alcohol. The fact that the fight itself was illegal would be avoided by making the match a "down river" bout, fought in a remote corner of Washington Territory on the Columbia River outside the jurisdiction of anyone interested in enforcing the law against such things.

Jumbo Reilly, who had probably already lost two secret fights against Campbell, was a "natural" fighter, not a boxer, but he wanted to put on a good show so he hired outside talent to train him for the match. His choice of trainer was Larry Sullivan, whom he offered $250 ($6,500 today) to come to Portland and get him in shape. Sullivan arrived on the Northern Pacific railroad, which completed the transcontinental link with Portland only two years before. He immediately lost his job, probably because, like Jumbo, he was also a natural fighter and had lied about having prize-fighting experience.

Above left: Larry Sullivan, who came to Portland as a boxer, turned crimping into a major industry. (*Oregon Historical Society*)

Above right: As a boxer and fire chief, Dave Campbell became Portland's hero. His funeral, after his tragic death in 1911, is still considered to be Portland's highest attended. (*Oregon Historical Society*)

Historian Barney Blalock says twenty-two-year-old Sullivan looked like "an overgrown schoolboy," but *The Oregonian* reported, "Sullivan's power is in his capacity to use foul language, in which art he is peer of any blackguard in the state at this time." The newly arrived Portlander wasted no time in picking a verbal fight with an *Oregonian* reporter and announcing that he could beat "nearly anyone." He became a regular patron of Old Joe Taylor's saloon, later known as the Willamette Palace, which had a full-sized boxing ring on the premises and was usually protected from the police as long as they enforced "Marquis of Queensberry rules," which meant boxers wore gloves among some other restrictions.

In order to support himself, Sullivan went to work as a sailors' boardinghouse runner. In 1885, Portland was just coming into its own as a transportation center. A decade into the grain trade with the insatiable British Empire and now connected with the transcontinental railroad, Portland was the second busiest port on the West Coast.

During the summer months, when the partially dredged Columbia River was impassable to ocean-going vessels, Portland had to rely on the port facilities of the older, smaller city of Astoria, 113 miles downriver. The picturesque city at the mouth of the Columbia had dreams of its own railroad that would allow it to become the "New York of the Pacific," but with John Mitchell in Washington D.C., Joe Simon in Salem, and the vast capital available to Henry Corbett and Henry Villiard in Portland, Astoria never stood a chance. Based on Portland's sleek fleet of steam tugboats, shipping became a major industry intertwined between the two cities.

The demand for labor created a brisk market for human beings, which was fed in many ways. Most often, workers were organized by ethnic group and managed by "labor brokers." For example, Portland merchants, such as Seid Back and Frank Woon, controlled a vast army of Chinese workers who only became more valuable when they were made illegal by the Chinese Exclusion Act of 1882. Other labor forces, like sailors, were organized by occupation.

Although steamships plowed the Columbia and Willamette, in the 1880s, it took sailing ships to cross the long distances of the sea. The sailing ships that plied the ports of Astoria and Portland came from all over the world, but most of them were British. The one thing they all had in common and could not do without was a crew of five to twenty-four "jack tars." By signing ship's articles, these sailors gave up their rights as free men for a specified term of service. They lived lives of hard labor, deprivation, and discipline with periodic "bust outs" on shore leave. The captain could rage and bellow, but without a crew to jump at his command, the ship would go nowhere.

Third and Burnside, a regular hangout for sailors and other transient workers, became Portland's most notorious intersection. (*Portland City Archive*)

James Turk, a U.S. Navy veteran of the Mexican–American War and San Francisco sailors' boardinghouse pioneer, is credited with bringing "crimping" to Portland and Astoria. "Crimp," an old English word for a fish trap, was what they called the "runners" of the boardinghouse system. The sailors' boardinghouse provided the needs of visiting sailors at inflated prices with easy credit. They were paid by taking the money the sailors received from signing onto a new ship, a fee known as "blood money." The vulnerable men who lived their lives being told what to do were easy prey for the crimps that sheared them of accumulated wealth and then sold them to the highest bidder. Most sailors worked for years without ever having a penny to their name. Larry Sullivan went to work as a runner for Turk, who had boardinghouses in both Astoria and Portland. The runner met ships as they came into harbor and befriended the crew with a combination of promises and threats. A talented crimp could get whole crews to desert as soon as a ship reached port.

Desertion was the illegal act that put sailors into the hands of the crimp. Once he left the ship, the sailor was deemed a law-breaker in debt to his protector, the crimp. Captains went along with the system mostly because they had no choice; when it was time to sail, they had to pay whatever price was necessary for a crew just to leave port. They had some financial incentive as well. A deserting sailor forfeited his wages for the entire voyage to the captain and there was no expense for housing and feeding the men during the idle time in port.

Sullivan, cultivating a gift for gab and an intimidating presence, was a natural crimp. The strapping young Irishman soon caught the attention of Bridget Grant, a widow and mother of eight, who ran a sailors' boardinghouse in Astoria. Soon, Sullivan was fast friends with two of her sons—Peter, age twenty-two, and John "Jack," age twenty-four. Jack had an affinity for sports, especially boxing. Peter was a more peaceful man, but he taught Sullivan how to turn brawn into gold then into political power. The three men formed a partnership (Sullivan and Grant Brothers) that would last for more than two decades and turn crimping into a major industry.

With a steady day job to support him, Larry Sullivan launched his prizefighting career. At the end of September 1885, he fought Mike Doyle in a Queensberry match at Old Joe Taylor's place for a purse of $40 ($20 put up by each fighter). Sullivan took seventeen rounds of punishment before he called it quits. Although he lost, Sullivan continued to brag of his prowess, offering to beat anyone who could match his $200 bet. Tom Ward, another crimp from Astoria, was eager to take "the blower" (as the hostile *Oregonian* called Sullivan) up on his challenge, as soon as he could raise the money.

In November 1885, Portland had its "Fight of the Century" when the *Police Gazette* lightweight champion of the world, Jack "Nonpareil" Dempsey, came to town to fight Portland's undefeated champion Dave Campbell.[2] The second event would be the long-anticipated fight between Larry Sullivan and Tom Ward, London rules. Betting was heavy in favor of Campbell and local sportsmen were disappointed, and much poorer, when the champ knocked out "Our Dave" in only four rounds.

The Oregonian published strident editorials decrying the brutality of the pugilistic sport and calling for its suppression. In the same editions, they regularly printed long columns describing the fights in vivid, gruesome detail. The bare-knuckle fight between Sullivan and Ward lasted almost 100 minutes. London rules allowed huge leeway in fighting methods, including the use of spiked shoes. Sullivan and Ward held grudges against each other, and both men, probably due to exhaustion, committed repeated fouls. *The Oregonian* said the audience was disgusted by the brutal spectacle, during which blood flowed freely, teeth were knocked out, and the men's faces were beaten so badly they looked like raw meat, but many of them stayed until the bitter end, when Sullivan lost on a technical foul for eye-gouging in the seventy-seventh round. Again, Larry Sullivan lost a fight, but he proved that he was not the coward that *The Oregonian* had called him. He could take all the punishment Portland had to give.

Sullivan continued to fight from time to time, including a legendary exhibition bout with Dave Campbell in 1890, but most of his matches were with pugs known for "throwing" fights, like Frank Silva. Sullivan's energy went mainly into his crimping career, where his "fistic" skills were equally valuable, and by 1888, Sullivan and Grant Brothers were well-known in Astoria. Sullivan had also established himself in Portland where he kept a small boardinghouse with a man named D. W. Pratt.

In June 1888, Sullivan met the bark *Kitty* as it came into port and spirited away its small crew of five Japanese sailors. It was a "happy accident" that, although it cost Sullivan a $150 fine, it also set him on a course to become the most powerful boardinghouse master in the city. The *Kitty* was a decrepit ship launched in 1856, owned by William Dunbar, who also ran a wholesale grocery business in Portland. Dunbar's silent partner was Jonathan Bourne, Jr., a Portland attorney and investor who was a rising star in the powerful Republican Party.

Everyone, including *The Oregonian*, warned Sullivan that he should leave locally owned ships alone, but he was not listening. The *Kitty* was not a happy ship. Her decaying condition was dangerous for those who worked on her; on a previous visit to Portland, first mate Andrew Clark nearly lost both legs when a bolt pulled out of the rotting forecastle and he was struck by a flying hawser. The ship made regular runs between Portland and Hong Kong. Later, as the owner of the notorious *Haytian Republic*, Dunbar specialized in smuggling illegal workers and opium. On her return voyage to Hong Kong, the *Kitty* was scheduled to carry a group of deported "lepers" who were expected to resist returning to China.

The crew of the *Kitty* deserted twice as Sullivan attempted to negotiate a better deal for them. Dunbar refused to negotiate, however, and he caused Sullivan just as much legal trouble as he could before sailing with a new crew. The five Japanese sailors, one of whom spoke English and went by the name of "Mike," became a small *cause célèbre*, gaining equal measures of sympathy and derision as *The Oregonian* called them variously "slippery little Japs" and "forlorn Japs."

Dunbar's partner, Jon Bourne, was from a textile manufacturing family of New Bedford, Massachusetts. After leaving Harvard under mysterious circumstances, Bourne took a sea voyage to the remote island of Formosa, where he was ship-wrecked for several weeks before finally washing up in Portland in 1878. Admitted to the Oregon bar in 1881, the practice of law was not Bourne's highest priority. His investments in mining, shipping, and other commercial enterprise and activism within the Republican Party took up most of his time. His true passion was having a good time, so much so that historian Finn J. D. John called him "Portland's municipal rascal."

In combination with political boss "Little Joe" Simon, Bourne became an influential voice in the Multnomah County Republican Party as well as police commissioner. He was a "ward heeler" in Portland's Second Ward, bounded by Everett Street in the south and Savier Street in the north and including most of the "Whitechapel" district, which was the North End neighborhood that became synonymous with vice and violent crime. Larry Sullivan controlled a large group of transient sailors who could be counted on to vote however they were told, as many times as they could. He became an important piece in Bourne's elaborate game of power.

Sullivan learned the lessons of the *Kitty* affair and was soon using the police and the courts against his rivals. In Astoria, Sullivan worked in coordination with Police Chief William Barrie, who got rid of "undesirables" by turning them over to crimps and shipping them off to the far corners of the world. In the most infamous case, Larry Sullivan received the "blood money" for shipping Darius Norris, a Clatsop County farmer who owned a valuable land claim not far from Astoria. Historian Barney Blalock tells, in *The Oregon Shanghiaers,* how Norris was framed on a murder charge, shipped off to sea and stripped of his property. In the process, Sullivan learned how to manipulate the authorities to increase his own power.

Sullivan became a familiar figure in Portland, as Barney Blalock says, "in his swell suit … strutting confidently about his illegal and immoral business as if he were a banker." Sullivan may have tried to look respectable, but his temper, enflamed by alcohol, was hard to control and hard to miss. After several foul-mouthed, brutal street fights, Sullivan became a figure of fear in the North End, but ultimately, that image was good for business.

Portland politics in the 1890s was dominated by a fight between factions in the powerful Republican Party.[3] Sullivan and his partner, Peter Grant, had political ambitions, and through their contact with Jon Bourne and membership in the Acme

The vehicle used for a paddy wagon changed over the years, but "Old 99" was used well into the 1960s. (*Portland City Archive*)

Republican Club, they gained influence through their ability to "deliver the vote" among other things.

The primary election of April 1890 was a bitter contest between a slate of candidates put up by Simon and another supported by Senator John Mitchell. Rampant multiple voting was noticed in all precincts, but especially in the Second (North End) and Third (Tenderloin and South Portland) Wards. According to *The Oregonian*, the Second Ward, where Larry Sullivan had his operation, counted more than 1,100 Republican votes in a district that had only 515 votes (total) in the previous election. *The Oregonian* concluded that "more money was used in the primaries than has ever been used in a primary election in Oregon before."

The paper reported the pay for votes: $2.50 early on, falling to $1 as the day progressed. The pay for "herders" and "strikers" was $25 to $50, with some earning up to $100 per day. According to *The Oregonian*, "some of them were the most depraved of the city's scum. The more votes they controlled the more they were paid." An anonymous election worker of the time told the paper, "You cannot carry an election unless you use money."

The world of crimping was in turmoil as Jim Turk lost his grip. Independent runners such as Joseph "Bunko" Kelley encroached on the established crimps. Sullivan had more success as a street fighter than he ever had in the ring and violence was frequent. Kelley went to work as a runner for Sullivan in 1891 and in 1894 was convicted of the murder of George Sayres.[4] During the politically charged trial, Sullivan made sure Kelley would serve a long sentence, putting away an unreliable friend. One by one Sullivan's rivals died (James Turk in 1895) or went to prison. By the end of the century, when he opened the ironically named Hotel for Sailors and Farmers and the luxurious gambling den known as the Portland Club, Sullivan was the unrivaled boss of crimping in Portland. According to historian Barney Blalock, he also owned several saloons and a dancehall.

The open corruption did not go unnoticed. In 1891, the Committee of 100, a reform movement uniting Republicans and Democrats who believed that corrupt government was bad for business, elected Henry Corbett as its president. The Committee's main purpose was to win the vote for city consolidation that would bring East Portland and Albina into Portland. In the process, pressure for reform helped them elect William Mason as mayor. Corbett, who owned the city's largest retail liquor store and the Arion gambling club, found rampant vice to be an uncomfortable subject, but the public clamor was too strong and he got behind the "anti-vice" movement, which was becoming popular.

Mason, up against impossible odds and faced with one of the worst economic depressions in history in his second term, made no headway in reforming city government or suppressing vice. The split in the Republican Party created a vacuum filled by the new mayor, George Frank, in 1894. Frank climbed the rungs of the Republican machine with support from Joseph Simon and then quickly turned on him, throwing his support to the rival Mitchell faction. Portland has had several corrupt mayors, before and since, but few have created the chaos that Frank achieved. He reorganized the police force, firing anyone who showed the smallest sign of disloyalty to him and taxed every city employee for his political fund. George H. Williams, one of Portland's more corrupt mayors, thought Frank was "an infernal scoundrel."

Portland has always been known as a "wide open" town, where anything goes in the "vice" fields (sex, liquor, drugs, and gambling). This has never been truer than during the term of Mayor George Frank. After two years of it, the casual corruption of the "Simon Machine" and Mayor DeLashmutt seemed quaint and a much better alternative. The "gambling and saloon interests" were not willing to let go of power, though. Mayor Frank controlled the machine "Little Joe" Simon built, and he pushed it to the limits. The primary election held in April 1896 was the most violent Portland has seen yet.

The "taxpayers" of Corbett's Committee of 100 united with Simon and Harvey Scott of *The Oregonian* who dubbed their opponents the "tax-eaters." Turnout was heavy with large crowds around the polling spots all day. Some 6,500 votes were counted, electing 124 delegates to the convention the following week, which would pick slates of candidates for city and county offices. With overwhelming voter turnout, Frank decided voter suppression was his only chance. *The Oregonian* reported, "scenes at the majority of the polling-places was [*sic.*] without parallel in the history of the Northwest. The entire police force of the city was devoted to the use of the ring." Police officers and "specials" surrounded every polling place and arrested and harassed the crowds who tried to get in to vote. According to *The Oregonian*, they "intimidated voters, threatened and even assaulted judges, and abetted and connived in violence, fraud and outrage." In the end, the "taxpayers" won, and, as *The Oregonian* said, "No one was killed."

The voting wards had changed slightly since 1891, and there were more of them in the expanded city that covered both sides of the river in 1896, but the voting results were startling in some of them. In the Second Ward, where "pandemonium reigned all the afternoon," Larry Sullivan's operation, which supported Simon, was effectively shut down and less than three hundred votes were counted where 1,100 were counted in 1891. Sullivan's reaction to his arrest at the opening of the polls has become an important part of his legend.

The Second Ward polling place was at Sullivan's Sailors' Home (115 North Second) and he opened the polls that morning ready to deliver for the "taxpayers." Captain Belcher of the police bureau, armed with an old warrant for perjury, arrested Sullivan, but as he escorted him away from the poll, Joseph Simon personally intervened, offering to pay $1,000 bail. Belcher insisted that bail could be paid after Sullivan appeared in police court. Suddenly, a group of sheriff's deputies, county employees still under control of Simon's machine, surrounded Sullivan, and "after a desperate struggle pushed along by the crowd," Sullivan made it into his house, which also happened to be the polling place. He went upstairs and "appeared at an open window with a wicked looking shotgun." Sullivan threatened the crowd with his gun and yelled, "I will shoot any man who tries to take me." Voting was difficult the rest of the day, but Sullivan did not shoot anyone.

At the end of the day, Sullivan surrendered and paid $5,000 bond on a charge of intimidation. One shot was fired, when a sheriff's deputy named Roberts drew his pistol and was knocked to the ground. Roberts was hurt. One African American voter lost his ear in a fight with another black man, "neither of whose names could be learned" according to *The Oregonian*. Violence occurred in most wards, including an infamous episode in Albina where police broke down the door of the polling place assaulting and threatening to arrest the election judges. The "taxpayers" may have won the day, but Republican power suffered, and Democratic Governor Sylvester Pennoyer was elected mayor.

Sullivan's loyalty to Simon was not forgotten and his power continued to rise, especially as he courted Mitchell's largess, playing the two political bosses against each other.

His monopoly on the crimping trade was indisputable after he destroyed the rival operation of "Mysterious Billy" Smith in 1903 with the help of the police and the state legislature. Larry Sullivan, with his fancy suit and house on Knob Hill, was at the height of his career. The Portland Club, which he ran with his partner Peter Grant, led the way in raking in gambling profits and gave him leverage over the corrupt city council that enabled Mayor George Williams' looting of the city treasury.

Henry Corbett died in 1903, signaling the passing of a generation. William U'Ren's Populist Party showed unexpected strength at the polls and with the passage of the initiative and referendum system of "direct democracy" they had a powerful tool for change. In 1903, a new city charter passed which would change the face of Portland politics starting in 1905. Power began to slip away from John Mitchell's political machine and Sullivan's criminal vote collecting mechanism. In 1904, the "local option" initiative brought out a huge prohibition vote, which, although it made little headway against City Hall, elected Tom Word, a dramatic, moralistic reformer as the new Multnomah County sheriff.

Getting no cooperation from the chief of police or the mayor, Word began raiding gambling dens in Portland, an unheard-of course of action for the county sheriff, in an effort to close down gambling in the city once and for all. *The Oregon Journal*, a new Democratic newspaper, ran startling exposes uncovering the corruption of city construction contracts and accusing Mayor Williams of collecting $80,000 from gambling operators. One of the *Journal's* exposés revealed that the Tanner Creek sewer had been built with no bottom to the sewer pipes, resulting in sewage seeping up from the ground in several neighborhoods. The disgusting revelation was nearly the last straw for Mayor Williams, but when he was indicted in January 1905 for dereliction of duty for not enforcing the gambling laws, it became clear that the corrupt machine that had been in control for nearly two decades was finally reaching an end.

By 1914, new technology replaced sailing ships and the demand for sailors decreased, signaling the end of the crimping business. (*Portland City Archive*)

Larry Sullivan saw the writing on the wall and tried to change with the times. In 1904, he sold his interests in sailors' boardinghouses and the Portland Club. He claimed that he was retiring from politics and business, but it was merely a ploy. His political ambition was as strong as ever and he had plans for the important city election of 1905. When U.S. Marshal Jack Matthews was stripped of office and Senator John Mitchell was convicted of perjury early in the year, the last nail was driven into the coffin of the "Mitchell ring." New voting regulations, requiring voters to come to polls with six "freehold" witnesses to verify their right to vote, proved that things would be different in Portland. In addition, the 1905 primary would be the first "direct primary," in which voters would vote for candidates for office rather than delegates who would pick candidates at a convention.

Sullivan struck a populist note when he announced his candidacy for City Council in 1905, saying that he would buy school books for all the children in the Second Ward if he was elected to the council, "even if I go broke," he stated. Historian Barney Blalock pointed out that Sullivan was unlikely to go broke buying schoolbooks in a neighborhood heavily populated by single men and working girls and few children. Sullivan also tried to position himself as a reformer, saying that Sheriff Word could never stop gambling in the city because he did not even know when or where it was occurring. Sullivan implied that as a "former" gambler, he was in a much better position to control vice.

Yet controlling vice was not Sullivan's priority. For mayor, he supported Fred T. Merrill, who was vacating the Second Ward council seat, and his campaign for a "wide open" town, which would virtually legalize all forms of vice in the North End, officially cutting the city in on the enormous profits available. The election was held just days after the opening of the 1905 Lewis and Clark Exposition, focusing national attention on Portland and the new "Oregon system" of democracy. The voting reform reduced turnout to the bare minimum and made it virtually impossible for working people to vote, unless they could bring six men who owned property to the polling place to vouch for them. Those who managed to cast votes signaled the end of "machine politics" and the "saloon ticket," by electing Democrat and respected physician Harry Lane decisively to fill the newly powerful position of Mayor.

Sullivan had been fortunate in his timing when he sold his interest in the Portland Club. Just a month later, Sheriff Word raided the club and arrested Sullivan's ex-partner, Peter Grant, for gambling. Barely acquitted at his trial, Grant left town for Tonopah, Nevada. When Sullivan was defeated in his bid for City Council, he had few ties to hold him in Portland and he soon followed his old partner to the drier climes of Nevada.

It was not the last Portland would hear of Larry Sullivan. Just about one year later, news came from Nevada that Sullivan and the Grant Brothers had struck it rich and formed the L. M. Sullivan investment company. Sullivan took advantage of his new reputation as a "financial genius" to promote the historic Gans–Nelson fight held in Goldfield in September 1906. Tex Rickard, the legendary boxing promoter, was called in to get things rolling and Sullivan acted as "financial agent" for Joe Gans, the first African American world boxing champion. Sullivan's job was mainly handling bets, but he probably had a hand in organizing the crowds of miners who threatened to riot whenever negotiations for the fight hit a snag. His involvement probably generated the rumors circulating that the fight was fixed.

In 1907, the Merchant's Bank of Reno Nevada collapsed when the L. M. Sullivan Investment Company failed to make a payment on a $400,000 debt. The resulting scandal revealed that the whole thing had been a Ponzi scheme from the start and nearly drove the state of California, which had invested heavily, to bankruptcy. Sullivan fled to Mexico, where he lost what little money he had left on a mining scheme, before returning to Los Angeles, where he was arrested for selling Mexican lottery tickets. He stayed in southern California for a few years and was involved in the *L.A. Times* bombing case, as an "investigator" for the defense. Of course, Sullivan had no experience as an investigator, but he did have experience in jury tampering, which attorney Clarence Darrow was accused of.

In 1916, humbled and nearly broke, Larry Sullivan returned to Portland, investing in the Friars' Club near Milwaukie. Prohibition was underway in Portland and soon Sullivan was out of business and his liquor cache confiscated. In a deal with the judge, Sullivan avoided jail on the condition that he take a job and pay a hefty fine. He took a job as a security guard at the new shipyard in North Portland where he died in 1918 at the height of World War I. His old enemy, *The Oregonian*, ran a glamorized obituary telling a mostly fictional story of Sullivan's life and calling him "a typical character of the West."

5

Unorganized Crime

… the city lay in the grip of business interests, gamblers and thugs.

Gordon Dodd

Three days after Portland celebrated the end of the Great War, in November 1918, Multnomah County Sheriff's Deputy Frank Twombly sat on his motorcycle just south of the Interstate Bridge in North Portland. Twombly joined the Sheriff's Department six months before as part of the first "speed squad" to monitor traffic coming into the city from Washington across the Columbia River on the new bridge. He and his partner, Jack LaMont, discretely watched the cars with a sharp eye from behind an advertising billboard next to the Standard Oil filling station at the corner of Vancouver Rd. and Darby St. Shortly after 11 p.m., a dark gray Hupmobile sped by, heading south.

"There's a good one," Twombly laughed to his partner. LaMont tried to kick start his motorcycle to give chase, but the engine sputtered and would not catch. "You chase him, Frank," LaMont said, "I'll have my machine fixed by the time you get back." Twombly took off after the speeder.

After nearly two years of war, Portland was finally experiencing an economic boom. The European war created a recession in Portland as foreign trade fell off and labor trouble paralyzed the lumber industry. When the U.S. entered the war in April 1917, the government nationalized logging in Washington and Oregon, destroying the I.W.W. logging union. This move got Portland's lumber mills working again, relieving the high unemployment that plagued the city. New shipyards opened in North and South Portland to supply ships for the war effort and 25,000 people flocked to the city to fill the jobs. With industry running twenty-four-hour shifts, Portland became a round-the-clock city as businesses stayed open to accommodate the needs of shift workers.

The streets were still crowded with people at nearly 11.30 p.m. when Twombly finally caught up with the speeding Hupmobile near the corner of Union Avenue (now Martin Luther King Jr. Avenue) and Portland Boulevard (now Rosa Parks Boulevard). Several people watched as Twombly came alongside the dark sedan and motioned for the driver to pull over. At least one witness saw the driver's hand, holding a pistol, extend out the

Jack Laird considered himself a criminal genius, but he never had good luck on the jobs he pulled. (*Oregon State Archive*)

window, and fire three shots at the pursuing officer. One of the bullets struck Twombly in the side, passing through his heart and both lungs. The motorcycle wobbled before hitting the curb and spilling the mortally wounded deputy into the street where he lay in a motionless heap.

Twombly never knew it, but just minutes before, the driver of the car had robbed the tollbooth on the Interstate Bridge. As the fleeing car disappeared to the south, people rushed to help the dying "speed cop" and the biggest manhunt in the history of Portland, up to that time, began.

The man the whole city was looking for was twenty-three-year-old Jack Laird (real name John Knight Giles) who hid out at the Dennison Apartments on Southeast Belmont Street with his lover, Augusta "Amy" Carlson, before fleeing to Seattle. Recently released from Washington State Prison in Walla Walla, Laird arrived in Portland in September 1918 with the plan to become the mastermind of a criminal gang. Things had not gone well for Laird and Twombly's murder came from his desperation.

Born in Tennessee, on February 16, 1895, Laird moved with his family to Everett, Washington, when he was a child. His parents divorced in 1910, and at the age of fifteen, Laird ran away from home, taking a job with a survey crew in British Columbia. An intelligent young man (his I.Q. measured above average at 116), Laird quickly mastered the use of survey equipment. While working in Canada, he began reading the works of philosopher Friederich Nietzsche, whose writing was just becoming popular in North America. From his reading, Laird got the idea that he was a "superman" above the morality of normal humans. By the time he was nineteen, Laird decided that working for a living was boring and his destiny was to be a criminal mastermind.

Returning to the United States Laird pulled off his first major crime in Centralia, Washington, just a few days after his twentieth birthday in February 1915. He successfully robbed a saloon, but he had a hard time getting away. Taking a local doctor hostage, Laird ordered the man to drive him out of town. After driving a few blocks, the doctor tried to take the gun away from the nervous young criminal. Laird fired several shots at his hostage before fleeing. The doctor was unharmed, but Laird was picked up a few hours later and sentenced to four years for armed robbery.

The prison in Walla Walla was a good training ground for the ambitious young criminal. Laird did well in prison and was released early in August 1918. A month later, he pulled off the most successful crime of his career—single-handedly robbing the Great Northern Railroad near Mulkilteo, Washington. He made what seemed to be a huge haul, escaping with more than $76,000 ($500,000 today) worth of Liberty Bonds and certificates. Laird was never lucky in his crimes and nearly $70,000 of his loot was non-negotiable, worthless to him. He netted only about $6,000 from the job and headed for Portland.

Portland's reputation as a "wide-open" city made it a welcome place for criminals to hide out. Two years of alcohol prohibition created great opportunities for illegal profit and Laird decided to go into the bootlegging business. He used some of his money to buy two large Hupmobile sedans and hired a couple of local criminals, Jerry and

The Interstate Bridge opened to traffic in 1917. In 1919, it was the scene of one of Portland's most disturbing crimes. (*Portland City Archive*)

George Noltner, to drive to California, where liquor was still legal, and bring back a carload. Laird made his headquarters at the Dennison Apartments, at Southeast 34th and Belmont, and began collecting camping gear and firearms. Evidently, Laird was planning to become self-sufficient somewhere outside the city because he also bought surveying gear and a portable machinist's kit. His shopping spree eventually took him to the Olds, Wortman, and King Department Store downtown, where a pretty salesclerk named Augusta Carlson caught his eye.

Amy, as Augusta preferred to be called, worked in the millinery department and had gained a great reputation, providing stylish hats for the wives of some of Portland's most prominent men, including William M. Ladd, the city's wealthiest banker and heir to the Ladd fortune. Laird stalked the pretty, young salesgirl and managed to follow her home to the Hillcrest Hotel, where he rented a room and started to court the young widow. Amy's first husband killed himself three days after their divorce was final and she was already engaged again to a local doctor, but the dashing young train robber swept her off her feet. Three days after they met, she moved into Laird's apartment on southeast Belmont with the promise they would be married soon.

Amy did not mind that Jack's money came from train robbery, and she joined his shopping spree, spending a great deal decorating his apartment. Laird planned to make a good score from illegal liquor, but he also planned a much more ambitious crime. Gathering information from Carlson about her wealthy customers, which she was more than willing to share, Laird composed a list of men he could kidnap and hold for $50,000 ransom each. His list included William M. Ladd, "millionaire lumberman" Frank J. Cobb, president of the Oregon and Washington Railroad and Navigation Company, J. D. Farrell and his attorney, Arthur C. Spencer. Amy had delivered hats to their wives and gave Laird information on each of their homes.

When the Noltner brothers returned to Portland in November 1918, they brought bad news with them. Their car, loaded with booze from California, was stuck in the snow in Mackenzie Pass, far southeast of Portland, and they would not be able to deliver Laird's liquor until the spring thaw. Short of cash, Laird ramped up his kidnapping plot. Using rubber gloves so he would not leave fingerprints on the typewriter keys, Laird typed a long letter of instructions and self-justification. Pretending to be part of a large gang with kidnapping experience all over the country, Laird signed his epic letter "nameless *et al.*" With little money left from the Mukilteo robbery, Laird put his kidnap plot into motion on November 19, 1918.

Not trusting his unsuccessful partners, the Noltner brothers, Laird hired a jitney driver named Kid Maples to drive him around. A jitney was a private car used as a taxi, and Laird told Maples he had important information that would need to be rushed to Salem after he made several stops. Laird never seemed to realize that his talent was for writing and not planning crimes. He and Maples stopped at all the houses on his list, starting with the Ladd home, but Laird's planning was faulty. He never learned his targets' schedules, and none of them were home when he arrived. His elaborate kidnapping plot was a failure before he could even start. After a frustrating day of driving around, Laird must have been in a foul mood and nearly broke when he arrived home.

Falling back on train robbery, his only successful crime to date, Laird bundled Amy Carlson into his Hupmobile and drove to the Vancouver railroad station. Carlson later testified that she and Jack Laird spent quite a while in the parking lot at the train station, looking for a weakness he could exploit, but the station was a military installation at the end of the war and the guard patrol was heavy. Jack was carrying two guns on his body and one under the driver's seat. They left the railroad station in disappointment and Amy said Jack was nearly wild as they drove back to Portland. As they crossed the Interstate Bridge, Jack got the idea to rob the tollbooth and Amy waited in the car. She said she was afraid of him by that point because he had become so angry. He was only gone for about ten minutes and then suddenly they were driving south very fast. After he shot out the window, he asked her, "What have I done?" He panicked when she told him he had just killed a speed cop.

In his panic, Jack threw a raincoat out the car window. The laundry mark on the coat led the police to the apartment on Belmont where they found his detailed kidnapping plan. Jack and Amy fled to Seattle, but about a week later, they inexplicably returned to Portland where they were quickly discovered and arrested. Amy testified against Jack and later went into hiding for the rest of her life. Jack was charming on the stand. The jury laughed several times as he told a crazy story of how he had been "framed up" for the shooting of Twombly. Jack was not laughing when they convicted him of murder and sentenced him to life in prison.

Jack Laird rebelled under the strict discipline of Oregon State Prison, gaining a reputation as a troublemaker before finally settling down with a job in the print shop. A few years after arriving in Salem, Laird met another convict, Elliot "Mickey" Michener, who would be an important partner in his later career.

Michener, a career criminal who committed his first armed robbery in Philadelphia at the age of ten, entered the Oregon State Prison in 1926 after being convicted of two robberies in Portland with his partner, Dick Franzeen. Franzeen and Michener met in the Idaho Industrial School, a facility for incorrigible youth to which Michener was sentenced after stealing more than $12,000 from his own father. Michener, who grew up in poverty after his parents' divorce, had developed a habit of opportunistic crimes followed by extravagant spending sprees. Franzeen, a petty criminal, became Michener's loyal partner. In July 1926, shortly after their arrival in Salem, Michener and Franzeen escaped and were free for four days before returning to prison. After their punishment, the two men started working in the print shop, where Jack Laird was now the supervisor and editor of the prison magazine.

Between 1928 and 1931, Laird and Michener collaborated on more than two dozen action and adventure stories featuring their Old West character "Black Bill." The stories, published in *Short Story* and *West* pulp magazines, became extremely popular. Their editor, Roy de S. Horn, of Doubleday and Doran, estimated that the two men, who wrote under the name "Jack Laird," had a readership of more than 1 million and told the O.S.P. warden they could have a lucrative career as writers and become productive, law-abiding citizens if they were released. Jack and Mickey had other plans.

In the O.S.P. print shop, the three men immersed themselves in the art of typesetting and made elaborate plans for the future. Sentenced to eight years each for their Portland robbery spree, Franzeen and Michener became model prisoners and were released early in 1933. After a short visit with Mickey's mother in Spokane, the two partners went to Minneapolis, near where Franzeen's family lived. They funded their travel, when the need arose, with armed robbery, but they had much bigger ideas in mind. In Duluth, MN, they forced an engraver to make printing plates for $10 bills. When they returned

The Portland police formed the Motorcycle Speed Squad in 1915. Multnomah County, which had responsibility for the Interstate Bridge, followed suit in 1918. (*Portland Police Historical Society*)

Elliott "Mickey" Michener was a career criminal who pulled off his first robbery when he was ten years old. (*Oregon State Archive*)

to the West Coast in October 1934, they had a large stack of counterfeit money in their car. Visiting Mickey's brother, Ashley, in Everett, WA, Mickey purchased a gift subscription to the *Daily Herald* newspaper for his friend Jack Laird, still in prison in Salem. Near the end of October, Mickey took out a classified ad in a prearranged code, letting Laird know that November 7 was the day their plan would go into action.

Meanwhile in Salem, Laird continued to make prison officials believe he was reformed and trustworthy and he was included in a work-release program that allowed him to leave the prison for unsupervised surveying jobs. On November 7, 1934, he went on a job and did not return. Mickey and Dick picked him up in a new car and the three criminals headed for southeast Washington State.

The escape plan worked like a charm and Jack Laird must have been elated. His plan was to recruit a powerful gang and rob trains to fund a counterfeiting operation. Laird was a meticulous, often obsessive, organizer whose complicated plans were worked out in great detail. Although the stories Jack and Mickey wrote together have not been located, some of Jack's writing is available. Jack's letters and essays give the impression that Mickey was the adventurous storyteller, while Jack was adept at bringing his stories to life in fine detail.

The fatal flaw in Jack's planning was a lack of intelligence gathering. His crimes were usually doomed before they even started. For example, on December 29, 1934, Jack, Dick, and Mickey boarded a train near Bucoda, WA, with the intention of robbing the mail car. After walking the length of the passenger train, the three criminals were frustrated to find there was no mail car. They forced the train to stop at gunpoint and fled with no money for their efforts.

Their first train robbery was frustrating, but the Laird Gang was good at recruiting. As they moved east toward Utah, the three criminals gathered together some help, and on February 7, 1935, when they boarded a Denver and Rio Grande Western train outside Salt Lake City, as many as seven men participated in the crime. This time, the train had a mail car, but unlucky Jack fired a couple of shots in a confrontation with an obstinate conductor. Alerted to the robbery the postal clerks barricaded the door of the

Jack Laird had big plans when he broke out of the Oregon State Prison in 1934. His luck was never good, and he ended up in federal prison. (*Oregon State Archive*)

mail car, and when the robbers demanded they open up, they answered with gunfire. Once again, the Laird Gang was forced to retreat with no loot.

The gang moved on to Milwaukee, Wisconsin, where they held another engraver at gunpoint and forced him to create plates for printing $20 bills. They supported themselves with small armed robberies, taking a few dollars here and there, but they were frustrated in their aim to be successful robbers. The escape from Oregon State Prison got a lot of publicity and Jack Laird was soon picked up by the police in St. Paul, MN. Oregon wanted him back, but Laird first had to face federal charges of mail robbery. He was sentenced to twenty-five years and sent to McNeil Island Penitentiary in Puget Sound.

It is difficult to verify, but William Dainard, the man convicted of kidnapping nine-year-old George Weyerhaueser in Tacoma in May 1935, may have been a part of Laird's gang. Historian Bob McNulty, who has spent considerable time researching Elliot Michener's life, says that Michener and Franzeen participated in the kidnapping and that Michener wrote the ransom note in that case. Michener was sought as a suspect, but he was never charged with anything connected to the kidnapping. The transfer of the $200,000 ransom in that case shows the influence of Jack Laird in its convoluted instructions, but it is impossible to know for sure if Michener was involved.

Although Jack Laird was back in federal custody, Mickey and Dick remained free. Supporting themselves by robbing grocery stores and gas stations, the two criminals made their way back to Milwaukee, WI, where they hit on a new scheme. Breaking into a factory just after it closed, the two men discovered the company checkbook in the safe. Forging several checks, Mickey went out to cash them around town, while Dick stayed behind to answer the phone if skeptical businessmen needed confirmation. On December 18, 1935, Mickey was arrested passing one of the checks in a liquor store. Dick got away, but was picked up near Northfield, MN, a few days later.

Convicted of forgery, Michener and Franzeen were both sentenced to thirty-five years in the Wisconsin State Prison, but soon, they faced federal charges of counterfeiting and each received additional thirty-year sentences. Mickey went to Leavenworth Prison in Kansas, but Dick went to Alcatraz, the new "escape-proof" federal prison in San Francisco Bay. Jack Laird, after a failed escape attempt at McNeil Island, also ended up in the maximum-security prison, which would soon earn the nickname "Hellcatraz."

Purchased for the U.S. government by California's military governor, John Fremont, in 1846, Alcatraz became a federal arsenal in 1861 and was used to house Confederate POWs and civilian political prisoners during the U.S. Civil War. The fortified island remained a military prison, and during World War I, it was used to confine conscientious objectors. In 1933, Alcatraz became part of the U.S. Federal prison system, and in 1934, it opened as a maximum-security prison for prisoners who had earned the reputation of troublemakers or who had attempted to escape from other federal prisons. In 1941, Elliot Michener attempted to escape from Leavenworth prison and earned his ticket to Alcatraz. Mickey, Dick, and Jack were reunited, and "The Rock" would be their home for the next decade.

Mickey and Dick settled into their new role as gardeners. The two friends found fulfillment in their work of beautifying their stark surroundings and concentrated on appealing their conviction. Jack Laird had not given up his urge to escape. He worked in the prison laundry and with the military buildup on Angel Island after the attack on

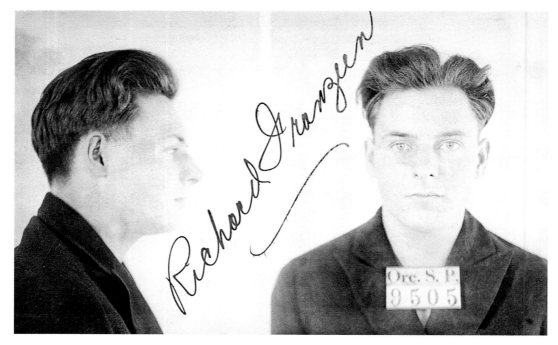

Dick Franzeen met Mickey Michener in the Idaho Industrial School. They remained partners for the rest of their lives. (*Oregon State Archive*)

Pearl Harbor, he began doing laundry for the army troops based on the nearby island. Laird, as usual, followed an elaborate plan that resulted in one of the most brilliant attempts to escape from the Rock ever recorded.

We do not know whether Jack Laird was involved in the 1943 escape attempt of Huron "Ted" Walters, but Walters disappeared from the laundry building where Laird worked. Jack must have at least observed the guards' reaction as the convict made his way to the shoreline, where he was captured. Alcatraz had the reputation of the toughest federal prison in the country and several men, both guards and prisoners, died in escape attempts during Laird's time on the island. Except for Theodore Cole and Ralph Roe, who made it into the water of San Francisco Bay in December 1937 during a storm and were presumed drowned, no escapee had ever made it off the fortified island. On July 31, 1945, Jack Laird changed all that.

Donning an army uniform, he had pieced together from laundry over the last four years, Laird disguised himself as a Sergeant and openly boarded a military transport boat that he hoped would take him to San Francisco. As the transport moved away from the dock at Alcatraz, Jack Laird, at the age of fifty, must have felt free for one of very few times in his life. In 1945, he had spent more than twenty-five years behind bars. The freedom was short-lived; as usual, failure to gather accurate intelligence doomed Laird's bold plan. The transport boat was not headed for San Francisco, where his uniform would have let Laird disappear into the crowd. Instead, it was bound for Angel Island, a secure army base. His

When Jack Laird was finally released from the Oregon State Prison in 1954, he had spent more than thirty-seven years in prison. (*Oregon State Archive*)

escape was noticed quickly by the guards on Alcatraz, and when Laird stepped off the transport, he was met by military police, who took him back into custody.

It would be another decade before Jack Laird would finally be released from prison. Mickey and Dick won their appeal in 1952. In the meantime, they had become master gardeners and soon patented some gardening tools. Released on parole, they went to work for a large nursery in Wisconsin. Mickey never forgot his friend still locked in a cell on the Rock. He wrote several letters to the warden of Alcatraz, who had become a friend and mentor, and to the warden of Oregon State Prison, where Laird was transferred in 1952. Mickey continually pleaded for Laird's freedom, claiming he had been rehabilitated. In 1954, Jack Laird won parole from his Oregon murder conviction and was released. At the age of fifty-nine, he had spent less than two years outside prison since his twentieth birthday.

Mickey had moved to El Monte, CA, near Los Angeles where he worked at Western Lytho Co. Jack got a job at the print shop there as well and soon the two old friends got involved in training racehorses. In 1962, Mickey and Jack patented a training system based on playing recordings of loud racetrack sounds for horses from birth. The patent gave the men secure income for the rest of their lives. Jack Laird lived in southern California, under his real name, John Knight Giles, until his death in 1979. Dick Franzeen continued in nursery work, recognized as "an expert in horticulture" by his employer, until his death in 1985. Elliott "Mickey" Michener lived until 1993 with only occasional cranky letters to the local papers to mark his passage.

6

ORGANIZED CRIME

Portland's biggest vice is her exaggerated virtue.

John Leader

It was about 2 a.m. on July 13, 1928, when a burglar pried open the back window of the general store in the rural community of Willow Creek, CA, not far from Eureka. Two men waited as the third man opened the window and another kept the engine running in the car nearby. The men who entered the store were yeggs, hardened criminals who specialized in armed robbery, burglary, and safe-cracking. Instead of opening the 200-lb safe, they wrestled it out of the store and into the trunk of the waiting automobile. Peter "Dutch Pete" Stroff, the mastermind of the job, was an expert safe-cracker, using "soup" (nitroglycerine), but with occupied houses near the store, he probably was afraid of drawing attention if he tried to blow the safe in place.

The robbers were smart to be cautious. Frank Graham, the manager of the store, was awakened by suspicious noises and looked out the window of his house across the street just as the car sped away. He quickly discovered the robbery and called the Lower Trinity Ranger Station in the nearby Trinity National Forest. As Ranger Robert Benson received the report, a small roadster with very bright headlights sped past the station. Benson called Deputy Sheriff Charles "Bud" Carpenter, who lived a little further along the road at a place called Burnt Ranch. Carpenter then called Oscar Hayward, a National Forest fire guard who lived nearby, and armed with rifles, the men took positions along the road waiting for the getaway car. They did not have long to wait.

The road was dark, and the bandits probably did not know they had been seen. At the wheel was William "Bill" Herder, a young car-thief and apprentice burglar from Portland. Along with Dutch Pete, the car also contained John W. Bishop, a career criminal known to Portland police as Stroff's partner in several crimes, and another man who was never officially identified. The fourth man was probably Leo Brennan, an escapee from Folsom prison wanted for a jewel robbery in Los Angeles.

The car had to slow for the hill near Burnt Ranch where Carpenter and Hayward waited. Deputy Carpenter stepped onto the running board and, backed up by Hayward,

Frank Kodat and Peter Stroff were released from Oregon State Prison in 1924. Although they had worked together for a few years, their partnership had just begun. (*Oregon State Archive*)

forced the robbers to stop. Carpenter pointed his rifle through the window of the car and barked, "Get out." Stroff and Bishop got out of the car on the passenger side and jumped Hayward, attempting to wrestle his gun away from him. One of the men in the car fired seven shots, killing Carpenter instantly and badly wounding Hayward. Hayward's rifle fired once, but no one was sure whose shot killed John Bishop, who collapsed by the side of the road. Herder stepped on the gas and the roadster disappeared into the gloom. Stroff, left behind, ran into the forest.

It was the last job in Dutch Pete's long career, but the gang he had built since he began operating out of Portland around 1906 would continue under the leadership of his protégé, "Shy Frank" Kodat, for nearly two more decades. Stroff, a German immigrant who entered the U.S. when he was twenty in 1894, served his first prison sentence for robbery in Montana in 1904. Soon after his release, he came to Portland and began recruiting yeggs for robberies. For the next twenty years, Stroff made Portland his headquarters as he and his gang robbed safes all over the west, pulling jobs in Oregon, Washington, and California. They were suspected of jobs in Utah, Nevada, Idaho, and Arizona, but Stroff had one rule he enforced with brutal discipline—no jobs in Portland, Oregon.

After the disastrous burglary, Dutch Pete wandered in the Trinity National Forest for several days before approaching the ranch of George Griner, nearly 12 miles west of Burnt Ranch. Hungry, thirsty, and exhausted, Stroff claimed that he was on a fishing trip with friends when he got lost, but he was unable to say where he had been fishing or who had been with him. Griner gave Stroff a meal and offered to let him rest on his front porch, but he eventually called the sheriff about the suspicious stranger.

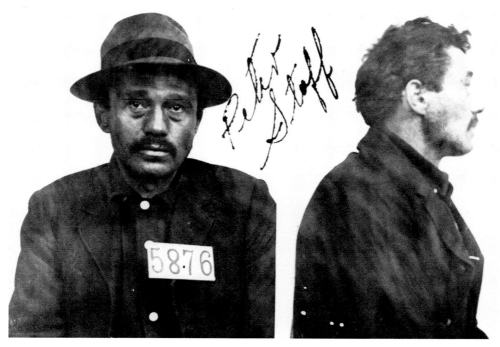

"Dutch Pete" Stroff went to prison for train robbery in 1908. When he got out in 1920, his robbery career was only beginning. (*Oregon State Archive*)

In the meantime, the sheriff had identified the dead man and learned from the Portland police that Bishop's usual partner in crime was Peter Stroff. Stroff refused to identify himself when the police arrived, but they had a good idea who he was. After twenty-four hours of interrogation, Stroff broke down, admitting his identity and identifying the driver as William Herder. The roadster used in the Willow Creek robbery was found abandoned near Oregon City and the manhunt focused on Portland.

Herder was "spotted" in Portland several times over the next few days, but he probably did not stay in town for more than a day. He was caught in New York City nearly five years later. Leon Brennan, who was never identified as a Willow Creek robber, surfaced in August when he kidnapped a farmer and his wife near Hood River, forcing them to clean out their bank account and hand over the cash. The couple then drove him to Vancouver, WA, where he disappeared. Several months later, Brennan was picked up for burglary in Los Angeles and returned to Folsom prison, where Stroff and Herder eventually ended up.

Dutch Pete was a hard worker, pulling dozens of burglaries in banks, post offices, and stores every year. Sometimes, things went wrong and Dutch Pete ended up in jail: in 1904 after a robbery in Lothrop, MT; in 1908 after the O.R.&N. "Chicago Express" train robbery near Portland; and in 1914 when he got shot during a robbery in Kelso, OR. Between 1904 and 1920, when he was released from the Oregon State Penitentiary, Stroff spent a total of fourteen years in prison. When he arrived in Portland in 1920, things had changed, but he needed to keep working.

Prohibition of alcohol started in Oregon in 1916, while Dutch Pete was still in jail. By 1920, Portland had become accustomed to illegal liquor and the general criminality it brought with it. George Baker, who served four terms as mayor between 1917 and 1933, had taken steps to make sure Portland had a reputation for law and order without slowing the supply of booze. Police Chief Leon Jenkins kept the lid on, raiding anyone who challenged the municipal bootlegging system or tried to use violence. Bobby Evans, an ex-boxer and Portland Boxing Commission "matchmaker," controlled the criminal element. Evans enforced discipline on, and profited from, local rackets and kept Al Capone and the east coast syndicate out of town. Dutch Pete, and his "no jobs in Portland" rule, was a natural for Matchmaker Bobby's system.

In 1920, shortly after the end of World War I, much of the wealth of the Pacific Northwest was tied up in Liberty Bonds and tucked into small-town banks, which relied on obsolete safes to keep them secure. Dutch Pete had been honing his safe-cracking skills and considered himself an expert on the use of explosives, especially nitroglycerine. Nitro, known to the yeggs as "soup," was the first commercially developed explosive and had been mass-produced for nearly a century. During World War I, large amounts of the explosive liquid were produced for the war effort. In 1920, it was not hard for a yegg to get his hands on some handy soup. With tools in place and a plan set, Dutch Pete had only one more thing to worry about—protection.

Jacob "Jake" Silverman was the man to see. His wife, Ewa, ran the family business—a boardinghouse/brothel on Southwest Third Avenue. Jake liked to drive. He provided transportation and connections to Matchmaker Bobby. After a four-year sentence in Folsom for robbery in 1904, Jake realized that the active, dangerous life of a yegg was not for him. Like his brother, Morris, who owned a small used jewelry store downtown, Jake preferred fencing and other low-profile crimes. He could make things easier for an ex-con trying to get on his feet. He may also have introduced Dutch Pete to his friend, Frank Kodat.

Jake Silverman was a pimp and driver who had solid connections to the syndicate that ran Portland. (*Folsom Prison Archive*)

65

Kodat earned his moniker "Shy Frank" by his inclination toward discretion, a trait that carried into every area of his life. Shy Frank was so discrete that he seems to have appeared out of nowhere. He was born in 1884 either in Bohemia or Illinois, a detail that changed depending on when a person asked him. Like many of his generation, Frank may have been born on the trip to America or shortly after arrival. There is no record of his arrival in America or of his birth; even the names of his parents are obscure. The first thing researchers learn about Frank Kodat is that he served a term in the Washington State Reformatory at Monroe, probably around 1900, under the name "J. Cody."

Dutch Pete was a natural teacher, and Shy Frank had been around. They made a good team, and the burglary of three banks in Willamette Valley towns south of Portland brought in $15,000 ($200,000 today) worth of Liberty Bonds. Liberty Bonds were traceable, but they could be passed if you removed the payment stamps and glued them to legally purchased bonds. It was a delicate work of forgery, but the Silverman brothers accomplished it easily with the help of Portland police officer Robert LaSalle. A federal investigation landed both brothers in jail temporarily in 1921, but the case eventually went nowhere. Legal fees and the occasional arrest were a cost of doing business, and they all understood that.

Rural Oregon has produced some of the world's great fortunes, but not for people who work for a living. When the I.W.W. union was dismantled by the U.S. government during World War I, it brought wages down in the lumber industry to starvation level. The drop in lumber prices after the war closed mills all over the state. In 1920, loggers and mill workers were lucky to have any job at any wage. Things had gotten so bad that even the Southern Pacific Railroad, another big employer in rural Oregon, was laying off. More than two-thirds of the SP's wartime employees were out of work. The picturesque little towns of the Rogue River Valley were begging for jobs and ripe for exploitation.

We do not know the cover story Dutch Pete and Shy Frank used when they checked into a hotel in downtown Medford, but they had to have one. Two city slickers from Portland in a flashy car would come under immediate police suspicion, and if their criminal records were discovered, they could be in big trouble. Two men from the city looking for investment opportunity would be welcomed with open arms, though, especially if they were generous with cash. Even in those days, when the roads through the rugged country of southern Oregon were unpaved, two men in a car could cover a lot of ground. From Gold Hill through Jacksonville, Phoenix, and Talent, the orchard-filled valley between Grants Pass and Ashland teemed with rural towns. Shy Frank and Dutch Pete must have visited them all before picking their target.

They struck after midnight on March 17, 1921, at the Talent State Bank in the sleepy little town of Talent, OR. Entering in the dark of night, the two yeggs set charges on the heavy vault door, but when the smoke cleared, the door still stood intact. The art of safe-cracking is learned by trial and error. Just because you know how to blow open one type of safe does not mean you can open them all. Frustrated in their attempts to open the vault, the yeggs had to make do with bags of pennies—$70 worth. It was hardly worth lifting.

The failed robbery alerted all the communities in the Rogue Valley that yeggs were in the area. Dutch Pete and Shy Frank had to lay low for several weeks as the heat cooled. They knew they would need more tools to open the tough bank vaults they were targeting, but with all the disgruntled SP employees and former employees, it was not hard for them to procure heavy tools from the local railroad yard workshop. When they tried again, they were prepared for anything.

A month after the Talent break-in, Rogue Valley bankers were still nervous. At the Gold Hill Bank in the little town near Grants Pass, William Wiseman was being paid to sleep in an observation room near the vault, a loaded rifle within his reach. About 1 a.m. on April 13, he was awoken by the noise of someone entering the back door. Sliding the cover back from his peephole, Wiseman saw two men drop a load of heavy tools on the floor in front of the vault. He took careful aim with his first shot but missed. Due to smoke from his weapon, the second shot was blind. Dutch Pete and Shy Frank ran to their car and disappeared in the dark.

Why they did not head for Portland that night remains something of a mystery. Maybe Frank was already starting to suffer from the arthritis that would plague the rest of his life and could not bear the thought of a long ride in the dark over rough and bumpy roads. Whatever the reason, the two yeggs were arrested in their Medford hotel the next day. They spent the summer in the Jackson County jail joking with reporters and claiming they were being "railroaded." In September, *The Oregonian* reported, "Influential friends of Strauff [*sic*], who is known as Dutch Pete, advised him to start serving his sentence and take his chances with the pardon board." It was good advice. Stroff and Kodat went to the State Penitentiary in Salem for a term not to exceed five years, and both received a conditional pardon on March 26, 1924, under three years later.

Frank Kodat returned to Portland shortly after his fortieth birthday. He contracted tuberculosis while in prison, and combined with his developing arthritis, Shy Frank was in constant pain. Fortunately, Jake Silverman had Frank's share of the proceeds from the Liberty stamp job waiting for him. Kodat bought a rambling building on Water Street, between the factories and the river at the east end of the Morrison Bridge and opened a hotel—or, more accurately, a flophouse. Frank let the word out that he was going straight and that he wanted to give back to the community by helping other ex-cons reintegrate with society.

Maybe "straight" was too strong a word. First of all, Shy Frank's new place sold booze. Illegal for nearly a decade in Oregon, there had never been a problem getting a drink in Portland. Bobby Evans' efficient operation, protected and abetted by the Portland police bureau, made sure that top-quality liquor was always available while keeping the city's reputation for strong enforcement of the law intact. Police Chief Leon Jenkins went along with a lot of things he personally did not agree with (for example, the growing influence of the K.K.K. in the police bureau), but he insisted on one thing: no violence. Strict "law enforcement" meant high liquor prices, which meant high profit for saloonkeepers like Frank Kodat. No more lifting heavy sacks of pennies for him. Dutch Pete, a decade older than Kodat and in much better health, was ready to get back to work.

Fortunately for Pete, Frank's plan to help out ex-cons gave him the opportunity to network with other yeggs, plan, and organize more jobs. Keeping to his "no jobs in Portland" rule and Chief Jenkins' no violence rule, Stroff and his friends were completely protected in the city. We will never know how many robberies they pulled, since Stroff was not caught again for nearly four years, but any burglary in seven states that involved a blown safe could have been done by Dutch Pete and his disciples. Soon, the word was out—when they released you from Salem, you had to go straight to Shy Frank's place. You could meet some interesting people there.

The dapper bartender, Abe Levine, could always get you a deal on a nice suit with all the accessories. He specialized in robbing men's clothing stores, a crime he went to prison for more than once.

John W. Bishop, one of the men who died at Willow Creek in 1928, was probably a regular at Shy Frank's when he was in town. Bishop, known as the "Telephone Box Bandit" in 1906 when Dutch Pete was getting his start in Portland, may have been Stroff's longest-term partner. A former telephone lineman, Bishop began his criminal life by stealing 1,500 lb of copper wire from Portland General Electric. The company had to drop charges when the witnesses against Bishop failed to appear in court. He got his moniker by using a skeleton key to loot the coin-boxes of the pay telephones that were beginning to appear around town. Bishop may have been an imaginative thief, but his real talent was strong-arming. He was arrested for assault more than once and in 1912 shot and wounded a Wobblie during a small riot at I.W.W. headquarters. He served prison sentences in Montana and Washington and was a known associate of Dutch Pete when he died.

William "The Boy Bandit" Herder was another regular at Shy Frank's. The son of a northeast Portland family of Russian immigrants, he got his moniker in 1920 when he was eighteen. Arrested by the Portland police for stealing a car, the young man admitted to heading a gang of teenagers responsible for stealing as many as one hundred cars and committing dozens of brazen burglaries, including two at his high school, Jefferson. Legally an adult, Herder went to the State Penitentiary for two years. He learned a lot. In 1922, days after being released he was discovered at the North Pacific Dental College on Northeast Sixth Avenue. He had almost finished "peeling" the safe.

Peeling is a labor-intensive process of finding a weakness and then tearing the safe apart by brute force. The steady pounding of Herder's sledgehammer announced his presence as he worked to remove the door and brought the police before he could finish. He jumped out an upper story window but was apprehended while hanging from the building's cornice before he could escape. Back in Salem for two years, Herder had

William "The Boy Bandit" Herder was the driver on the ill-fated Willow Creek robbery. (*Folsom Prison Archive*)

plenty of time to get to know Dutch Pete and Shy Frank. His naturalized citizenship was revoked in 1924 and Herder was deported. Working on merchant ships, the young thief never made it to Russia and was back in Portland in 1925, this time under a $1,000 bond to ensure good conduct. An auto-mechanic by training and a car-thief by inclination, twenty-three-year-old Bill Herder made a good driver for out of town jobs.

Shy Frank's place became a clearing house for information on burglary targets all around the region. Dutch Pete could take his pick of jobs and give advice on the ones he did not want in exchange for a cut. He had a large pool of yegg talent to choose from, and he could recruit whom he wanted for his jobs. In his case, it was nice to be untouchable.

The botched Willow Creek job brought a lot of unwanted attention, and when Della Hand, a troubled young woman from a Portland bootlegging family, started talking, it looked like Shy Frank might go down with his partner. Seventeen-year-old Hand, who had talked her way out of jail and into the Oregon State Hospital, claimed that she knew all about what was going on at Shy Frank's place. She said Dutch Pete was the mastermind and that Frank had participated in robberies of two banks in Eugene and the post office in Gresham. There were problems with Hand's story. For example, the post office in Gresham denied that it had ever been robbed. The banks in Eugene had been robbed, though. Shy Frank was picked up and sent to Lane County to face charges.

The case fell apart when Della Hand was released from the state hospital and brought to Lane County to testify against Shy Frank. When she got on the witness stand, Hand's story changed. Suddenly, she did not know anything about the robberies. She said she made it all up after reading about the Willow Creek robbery in the paper. No one really believed her, but what could they do? They dropped the charges against Frank, and he went back to Portland.

With Dutch Pete in jail in California, Shy Frank was left as the boss. Things slowed down under Kodat's leadership, or at least they seemed to. Bank and drug store burglaries did not stop, but there was nothing to tie Frank to them. He ran his boardinghouse

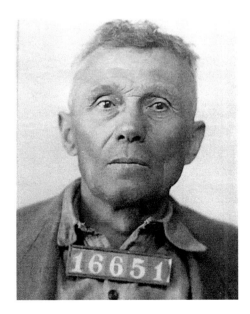

Peter Stroff was an old man when he went to prison for the last time for the Willow Creek robbery. (*Folsom Prison Archive*)

and speakeasy just like before and worked on building up a loyal organization to protect his interests.

Herschel "Jack" Crim was part of that organization. Crim's mother was a Modoc Indian and he grew up on the Klamath Reservation near Chiloquin, OR. A big, good-looking man with soulful dark eyes and a squashed nose, Crim started boxing in his youth. Jack was a ladies-man who always had a beautiful girlfriend on his arm and a wife at home. He joined Tex Salkeld's Portland list of multi-ethnic boxers in 1931 as the Indian fighter. Salkeld, whose popular fight card foreshadowed the later popularity of Portland Wrestling, followed Fred T. Merill's advice by providing the public "what it wants" and giving everyone, no matter which ethnic group they belonged to, someone to root for and to bet on.

Crim could be an extremely violent man. In 1931, on a visit home to Chiloquin for the Fourth of July, he was arrested for assault with a deadly weapon. The arresting officer had quite a bit to say in Crim's prison file. Under "Observations of Officials," he wrote:

> Crime, AWDW—Previous reputation, Bad.—Moral character, Not Good.—environment and associates—not good. Was armed and under the influence of liquor. Summary of crime: Got drunk and went on the warpath, for no good reason what-so-ever, and knocked a couple of men down, knifed one or more then went to Justice of the Peace, Jack Almeter, at Chiloquin, Ore. and threatened to beat him up. [*sic*.]

Jack was sentenced to three years, but Tex Salkeld had pull with Matchmaker Bobby, and Portlander Julius Meyer, a friend of Mayor Baker, was governor. On August 1, 1932, less than a year after his sentencing, Jack Crim was back in Portland, paroled to the custody

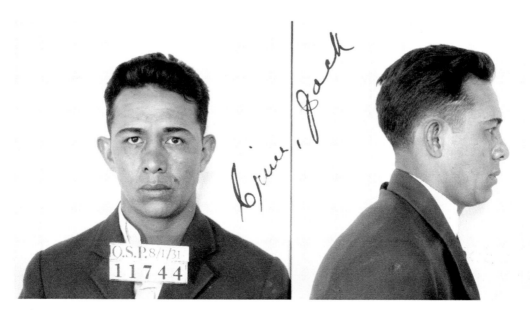

Jack Crim could be a violent man, but connections through boxing promoter Tex Salkeld and Frank Kodat mostly kept him out of jail. (*Oregon State Archive*)

of Leo Lomsky, another of Salkeld's boxers. Jack supplemented his income from boxing by working as a bouncer for various taverns and doing enforcement jobs for Shy Frank. He was most likely the gunman in the 1933 double-murder of Jimmy Walker and Edith McLain, a story I tell more fully in my book *Murder and Mayhem in Portland, OR.*

James "Jimmy" Walker, an ex-con from the Midwest newly released from the Oregon State Prison, said it was an accident when he took Shy Frank's gun away and shot him in the shoulder. Trouble had been brewing ever since Jimmy arrived, though. Many of the old-timers felt he did not show the proper respect to the boss, and he paid too much attention to Frank's girl, Edith McLain. There were various stories about how it happened, but everyone agreed on the ending. Shy Frank got a bullet in the shoulder and a lot of new pain. Jimmy and Edith ended up dead in a muddy ditch, across the county line, near St. Helens.

Jack Crim was picked up right away by the Portland police. He had blood on the cuff of his trousers and Shy Frank's gun at his apartment along with Edith McLain's purse. He got the blood on his clothes from a fight at his girlfriend's beer garden, where he worked as a bouncer, he said. He picked up the purse when he went to get the gun at Shy Frank's, she had left it behind. They held him on a charge of "ex-con in possession of a weapon," but soon released him. Jake Silverman's car was identified as the one that picked up Walker and McLain in downtown Portland and then was seen driving away from the scene of the murder. Silverman pled guilty to manslaughter and spent three years in Salem—the cost of doing business.

Not only does the Walker–McLain murder illustrate the efficient nature of Shy Frank's organization, it also shows how Portland's underworld was changing, becoming more sophisticated and ultimately more dangerous. In 1931, *The Oregonian* ran an article, eerily echoing an article on the same subject in 1908, in which Police Chief Leon Jenkins warned of the "alarming increase in crime in the last two months." Just as Chief Gritzmacher had warned the people of Portland twenty-five years before when Peter Stroff first arrived in Portland, Chief Jenkins blamed rising crime on the ex-convicts who flooded the city and called for stricter laws to control them. Jenkins complained that there had been twelve successful safe burglaries in April, a record in a city that saw only one to two safe burglaries a month when Frank Kodat's gang was strongest. In June, the chief said, the city was already on track to surpass April's record. Clearly, Shy Frank's control of the yeggs and his "no jobs in Portland" rule was slipping.

Leon Jenkins must have appreciated Shy Frank's discreet handling of the Jimmy Walker matter, with murder tidily kept offstage in Columbia County, but he did not like violence unless he personally felt the need to use it. Jenkins' relationship with Bobby Evans soured in 1932, but the chief never really felt comfortable in that relationship anyway. The political scandal over the special election that year, when Evans' men stole recall ballots from the election office, was bad enough, but the DePinto brothers bombing campaign to take over Tom Johnson's downtown gambling racket was the last straw.[1] Bobby Evans, his power broken, would spend the next several years in and out of court. His strongest supporters—Nick DePinto, Abe Weinstein, and Jake Minsky—went to jail for long stretches. Matchmaker Bobby would have to lay low for several decades before he could reinvent himself as one of Portland's colorful characters.

The whole thing was embarrassing for Mayor Baker too. He decided not to run for a fifth term. Leon Jenkins, who had been chief almost as long as Baker had been

Joseph Carson replaced George Baker as Portland mayor in 1933. The change in administration ushered in a struggle for control of vice in the city. (*Portland City Archive*)

mayor, knew his days were numbered as well. The new chief, Burton Lawson, was not a Portland cop, so he never knew what was really going on. The new mayor, Joe Carson, liked the power Baker had given to City Hall, but he was embarrassed by the graft involved and had to be cut out of the loop. It was a free-for-all and a guy like Shy Frank could only rely on his friends, people he had been working with for years and whose loyalty he could trust.

Shy Frank's stayed open, although there were occasional court appearances and OLCC fines. The cost of doing business. Jake Silverman was back in Portland and up to his old tricks by 1937. A new generation of organized crime was coming into power by then.

Al Winter, a Portland attorney connected to Jack Dragna's Los Angeles operation, got control of the "gaming wire." A national wire service that provided results of horse races and other sporting events all over the world was a valuable asset for a gambling operation. Winter used the power the gaming wire gave him to build a gambling and entertainment empire which included Portland's Pago Pago Room and Las Vegas' Sahara Casino. Jim Elkins arrived in Portland in 1937 as well. Elkins had a sadistic streak and he liked to prey on other people who made their living through crime, trying to outsmart them. He muscled Royden Enloe out of his coin-machine business and then began providing "protection" for operations like Shy Frank's.

Shy Frank managed to stay on the good side of both men. His health declined and he became more of a consultant than a boss, becoming more homebound, but he did not do too badly. Finally getting over the heartbreak of Edith McLain, Shy Frank married Dorothy Redecker on August 13, 1945. Shy to the last, Frank waited until he was sixty-one for marriage. Jake Silverman opened his own tavern in the North End, the Santa Fe on northwest 6th. He was working there the night he died of a heart attack in 1949, the same year his old buddy Shy Frank passed away.

7

Murder for Hire

Organized crime is nothing more than capitalism with the mask of respectability removed.

Dave Mazza

Portland was packed on the weekend of November 21, 1919. With the Shriners' convention and the annual stock show scheduled, the hotels in town were full. The Shriners Parade on Saturday would be one of the big events of the year with famed western lawman Sheriff Tilman D. "Til" Taylor, from Pendleton, leading the way on his tall white horse. The Benson Hotel hosted a delegation from Umatilla County, which represented the most important economic and political power in the rural part of the state to the east and upriver along the Columbia from Portland. Jasper N. Burgess, ex-state senator and recently appointed state highway commissioner, represented the sheep-raising interests. George E. Peringer, the largest landowner in Umatilla County, represented cattle-raising. E. P. Marshall, a prominent Republican Party activist from Pendleton, represented the wheat growers. All three men were friends of Sheriff Taylor and involved in the board of the Pendleton Roundup, Oregon's biggest annual rodeo. Burgess, Peringer, and Taylor had interests in horse racing as well.

The junket to Portland was a chance for powerful men to "let down their hair" and have fun in the wide-open town, but Portland was not as wide-open in 1919 as it had been, or would be again in the future. George Baker had only been mayor since 1917 and his police chief, Leon Jenkins, took office only days before the Shriners' weekend. World War I had ended a year before, but an influenza epidemic and the Red Scare kept tension high and discipline tight. Only ten days before, labor trouble resulted in an incident of mass murder and lynching in the Washington town of Centralia, less than 100 miles north of Portland. When Burgess and Peringer piled into E. P. Marshall's touring car with Lora Hastings, a Benson Hotel telephone operator, and her friends Elsie Babcock and Jane Shelton, they were out for a good time. Marshall headed out of town, going east along the Columbia on the Linnton Road.

Walter Banaster was one of the gunmen who robbed the Claremont Roadhouse in 1919. When he got out of prison in 1933, he seemed to have plenty of money. (*Oregon State Archive*)

The Linnton Road had been a "vice" destination in Portland since the 1870s when it was home to the Terminus Saloon, notorious for its African American prostitutes and reputation as a hangout for ex-convicts. Since about 1905, the Claremont Tavern, a rambling house on the bank of the Columbia River, provided food and drink to the "dry" community of St. Johns, just across the river. Outside Portland city limits in unincorporated Multnomah County, the Claremont became a popular goal of day trips for the burgeoning car-culture of Portland. Portland's roadhouses, which grew like mushrooms around the city in the decade after the Claremont opened, were frequent targets of anti-vice campaigns. Moralists objected to the "immoral" dancing and illegal gambling and they loudly denounced the roadhouses, especially after the gruesome drunk driving car accidents that plagued county roads around the drinking establishments.

In July 1919, the old Claremont opened under new management, advertising à la cart lunches, chicken dinners, and seafood served by the "boys just returned from service overseas." Miles Coakley, a U.S. Army private in the war, was the boss. Coakley specialized in re-habilitating notorious old places, converting them into "soft drink parlors" to comply with the anti-alcohol prohibition laws that took effect in 1916. That year, he re-opened the notorious Belle Hotel in Milwaukie, promising to run it in "an orderly manner." He had varying success with order at the Belle, he even ended up in jail briefly on a liquor charge, but Coakley was a "sportsman," as Portland likes to call its professional gamblers, and obviously had connections. His stay in jail was brief and *The Oregonian* was very discreet about his identity and background as it reported on the events of November 21, 1919.

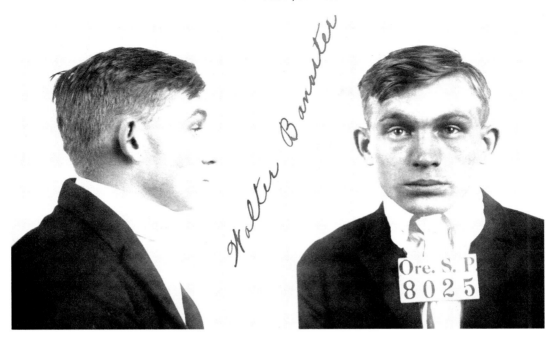

Walter Banaster in 1919. His role in the Claremont robbery established him as a connected member of the Portland syndicate. (*Oregon State Archive*)

With all the powerful people involved, *The Oregonian* was very delicate in its coverage of the shocking case. The news story implied that Marshall and his party had been on a sightseeing drive and merely stopped "for lunch" at the roadhouse. The reader has to wonder why the lunch break took place after 10 p.m. Although the party's table was crowded with ginger ale bottles, Marshall's checkbook and a pile of "football tickets," and parts of a meal that had been served, *The Oregonian* reported that they had arrived "only minutes before." Readers familiar with the history of the Claremont Roadhouse would not have to wonder if they added anything stronger to their ginger ale, or whether they were gambling. The roadhouse was crowded; more than twenty-five people enjoyed George Jackson's fried chicken and Charley Garing's piano playing. The Claremont advertised "banquets and dinner parties given special attention." The proprietor, Miles Coakley himself, probably escorted Marshall and his party of important men to their private dining room.

Three men took the last ferry from St. Johns at 10.20 p.m. It was about 10.45 p.m. when they landed near Linnton and made their way toward the Claremont. They knew their leader as Little Dutch, but he went under the name "Walter Banaster." He had been released from the Montana State Prison less than six months before after serving almost five years on an armed robbery charge. James Ogle was also from Montana and may have been in the state penitentiary, for horse theft, at the same time as Banaster, although he claimed he only met Little Dutch in Portland. Ogle would turn out to be an unreliable witness. "Dave Smith" is the name the third man went by. His real name was Eugene Roesel and he was a twenty-two-year-old drifter from New York. Usually referred to as an ex-convict, the only police record on him was a thirty-day sentence for vagrancy in Seattle in 1917. As they approached the roadhouse, the three men pulled their caps low and covered their faces with large handkerchiefs, pinning them in place with distinctive pieces of jewelry. One was a skull with jeweled eyes; another, the hear-no-evil, see-no-evil, speak-no-evil monkeys; the third pin was never mentioned or described.

Patrolman John Case of the St. Johns precinct noticed the three suspicious characters as they got off the ferry. He followed them at a discreet distance and watched as they covered their faces before they entered the Claremont. Drawing his pistol, he hurried around the building and into the cellar through the back door. The masked men went directly to the private dining room where E. P. Marshall entertained his friends. Accounts of what happened next vary considerably. All three of the masked men denied that they confronted Peringer and Burgess. Most of the witnesses disappeared as soon as the robbery ended and were not identified by the police. The eyewitnesses who remained could not identify which of the masked men was which, and there was a great deal of confusion about the jeweled pins they wore and what they looked like. One of the robbers took Miles Coakley at gunpoint into the basement, where the safe was, getting the drop on Officer Case and relieving him of his gun along the way. The "tall one" herded the customers and staff into the main room and relieved them of cash and jewelry. The third one forced his way into the private dining room, surprising Burgess, Peringer, Marshall, and their companions.

According to some witnesses Jasper Burgess, a veteran Shriner and practical joker, thought the robbery was a prank pulled by fellow Shriners. E. P. Marshall denied it, but some reported Burgess said, "Go ahead and shoot," when the gunman pointed his pistol at him. Whether he said it or not, the gunman did just that. Three bullets pierced Burgess' body, killing him instantly. Peringer jumped to his feet and tried to force the gunman out with the door. The gunman fired at least once more, hitting Peringer with a bullet through the paneling. Peringer stumbled out the door and died in full view of the frightened guests in the main room.

The three robbers escaped across the river in a rowboat stashed near the Claremont before the job. The victims said the robbers escaped with about $2,500 in cash and jewelry, but all three robbers later complained that they got less than $200 each. In St. Johns, they retrieved their waiting car and drove to a hideout in North Portland, not far from Peninsula Park. According to James Ogle's story, which changed every time he told it, Banaster complained that he had to "bump-off" somebody because he tried to fight. Ogle, the tallest of the three robbers, told many stories blaming both Banaster and Smith for the killings, before "coming clean" and saying he was the man who did the shooting. It turned out that Ogle, the main source of information on the Claremont Roadhouse case, could not be trusted to tell the truth.

Walter "Little Dutch" Banaster is most likely George Herman, born in New York City in February 1897 to German immigrants Joseph and Anna Herman. He used many names in his life and even changed the spelling of his last name to Bannister in the 1930s, so it can be difficult to trace him. He came to Portland after his release from the Penitentiary at Deer Lodge, MT, in the spring of 1919. He made connections fast.

Above: Patrolman John Case watched three men get off the last ferry from St. Johns and followed them to the nearby Claremont Roadhouse.
(*Oregon Historical Society*)

Right: James Ogle, a horse-thief from Montana, was the main source of information on the Claremont murders, but he could not be relied on to tell the truth.
(*Oregon State Archive*)

After the Claremont job, he and his accomplices went straight to a safe-house run by Vincent Murphy and occupied by Murphy's family. Henry Travers ran a still in the basement. The house was often occupied by armed robbers who had to lay low after a job. The address can be connected to many of the armed robberies and burglaries that occurred in Portland and surrounding areas in the 1920s. The men who used the place as a hideout—Frank Butler, James "Columbus Jimmy" Murray, George Welch, and Wallace Witzel among them—make up a who's who of crime from the era. The house was under the protection of a "fix." The fix was most often an attorney, like I. G. Ankelis, or a businessman, like Paul Ailes, who had influence with the police or with "Matchmaker Bobby" Evans, the boxing commissioner and close friend of the mayor who was just beginning to take control of gambling and bootlegging in Portland. The illegal function, of protecting law-breakers from prosecution, these "fix" men performed means that they kept their identity secret; it only came out when things went very wrong. We do not know who Vincent Murphy's fix was, but he had to have one.

Sheriff Til Taylor dropped everything to join Portland detectives in their search for the killers. "Underworld tips" sent the police directly to Murphy's house where they captured the three robbers the day after the crime. Law enforcement in Portland often seems like an exercise in theatrics, the Claremont Roadhouse case more than others. The three robbers were portrayed as desperate criminals, armed to the teeth and ready for a fight, but they were all docile when they surrendered and they cooperated with the police, each confessing to their role in the robbery, but denying their part in the shooting. Days later, all three of the Claremont robbers pled guilty to second-degree murder and received life sentences. Before the end of November, they were securely locked up in the State Penitentiary in Salem. The Claremont Roadhouse case passed into history as a robbery gone wrong.

The meaning of the Claremont Roadhouse case is only understood in context with other complex events. Til Taylor, the sheriff of Umatilla County, who participated in the hunt for the killers of his friends Burgess and Peringer, died several months later during a breakout from the Pendleton jail. It seemed to be completely unrelated to the events in Portland eight months before, but in 1935, Richard Patterson told his version of the story to Fred M. White of *The Oregonian*. Patterson revealed that a few days before the breakout, Frank Butler smuggled hacksaw blades into the jail. Frank Butler, a yegg with a long record of arrests, was connected to the gang that used Vincent Murphy's safehouse where Banaster and his accomplices hid out. The deaths of Burgess, Peringer, and Taylor left a power vacuum in eastern Oregon and the gambling world. Shortly after Taylor's death, Bobby Evans, the Portland gangster, began to extend his interests in eastern Oregon. By the 1930s, Hyman Weinstein, a close ally of Evans, was known as the "vice king" of eastern Oregon—a position he kept until the 1980s.

The Claremont killers adapted well to prison life. Ogle participated in sports, especially boxing and baseball. David Smith eventually took a job in the infirmary where he studied dentistry through correspondence courses. Walter Banaster, who always seemed to have plenty of money, studied radio technology and bought the latest equipment, which was delivered to his cell. All except Banaster had exceptionally bad luck, though. In 1922, James Ogle was shot to death by one of the prison's most violent guards, John Davidson. Davidson, who acquired the nickname "Slaughterhouse," killed at least three prisoners, two at Salem and one at Walla Walla, where he worked previously. In addition, Davidson was fired at least twice after charges of brutality were brought against him. David Smith died in 1927 after being hospitalized for influenza. The prison informed his family in New York that he had died of a "throat infection," but questions surrounding his death were never sufficiently answered.

While the Claremont killers were in jail, Bobby Evans increased his control of bootlegging and gambling in Portland in alliance with Mayor George Baker, a story I tell in detail in my book *Murder and Scandal in Prohibition Portland*. By the end of Baker's fourth term in office, Evans had control of most of the bootlegging as well as a good portion of gambling, prostitution, burglary, and armed robbery in Portland. With cooperation from Police Chief Leon Jenkins, Evans became one of the most powerful men in the city with influence in City Hall and the Police Bureau.

Portland Police Detective James Tackabery, one of the officers who arrested Banaster after the Claremont robbery, took a special interest in his case. He petitioned Governors I. L. Patterson and A. W. Norblad, as well as State Parole Officers Charles Pray and Dan Kelleher for leniency for Banaster. At Tackabery's urging, Judge William Gatens, who had sentenced Banaster to his life term, and Judge Walter Evans added their pleas for a pardon. Their petitions were unsuccessful until Julius Meier, a close friend of Portland Mayor George Baker and under the influence of Bobby Evans, was elected governor in 1931. In December of that year, Banaster's life sentence was commuted to twenty years. In March 1933, Banaster was released.

Little Dutch was a career criminal, and he wasted no time getting back to business. Less than three months after his release from Salem, he was picked up by the Portland police for carrying a concealed weapon. Things were changing rapidly in Portland in 1933. First of all, liquor was legal again; the easy money available from the sale of illegal booze was sharply limited. Also, George Baker was no longer mayor. He had been replaced by Joseph Carson, who was embarrassed by the criminality he found in city government. Carson did not really stop any of the criminal activity the city was involved in, but he forced it deeper underground. Police Chief Leon Jenkins had been demoted to inspector and put in charge of the night shift. Although Jenkins and other officers could still protect criminals, the benefit of protection was no longer something that could be assumed. Most importantly, Bobby Evans had lost his grip on the city. After a violent, overreaching campaign to increase his personal power (which I describe in detail in Chapter 9 and my book *Murder and Scandal in Prohibition Portland*), Evans was in disgrace, with his most active allies imprisoned. The resulting power vacuum left Portland unstable and violence was on the rise.

Banaster was released and there were no repercussions from his parole violation, but he obviously felt Portland was too volatile. The situation in the city created opportunities for someone willing to take bold action, but Walter Banaster decided to take advantage of those opportunities from out of town. He moved to Olympia, 100 miles north of Portland, the capitol of Washington State. Halfway between Portland and Seattle, Olympia was a small town with a clear power structure. Little Dutch was soon the proprietor of a "gambling resort" just outside city limits known as "The Wigwam."

The Wigwam became a popular hangout for high-stakes gamblers from all over the Pacific Northwest. Regular customers included Frank and Anna Flieder of Bremerton, WA, and vaudeville entertainers Eugene and Peggy Chenevert. In addition to such "high-rollers," criminals such as Portland bootlegger and pimp Jack Justice and Seattle

George Baker served as Portland mayor from 1917–1933 and kept tight control of vice in the city. When he left office, rival factions competed for control. (*Portland City Archive*)

hitman Leo Hall frequented Little Dutch's place. So did a heroin-addicted thief named Larry Paulos and his waitress wife, Peggy. With Walter Banaster's background, it is not unlikely that he helped broker contract-murder deals that resulted in two of the Pacific Northwest's most notorious crimes: the Portland murder of State Investigator Frank Akin and the Erland Point Massacre.[1]

In November 1933, Frank Akin, a forensic accountant assigned to investigate corruption in the Port of Portland and the Portland Water Bureau, was shot to death in his S.W. Portland apartment. Frank Butler's arrest in the same building (the Arbor Court Apartments) just months before Akin's murder is probably a coincidence. It does show that the building was being used as a safe house by another "fix," since Butler was wanted for more than one robbery and was arrested with a group of accomplices. The Portland police, under new Chief Burton Lawson, were baffled by the murder, although suspicion that Akin was killed to stop his investigative work was heightened by the disappearance of his briefcase containing a preliminary report and investigation notes from his Water Bureau inquiry. Although a previous attack on Akin, just days before Frank Butler's gang was arrested in a neighboring apartment, increased suspicion even more, the case remained unsolved. In the 1970s, historian Kimbark Macoll considered the Akin murder one of Portland's most significant unsolved crimes.

The Erland Point Massacre, four months later, on Washington's Olympic Peninsula, was called the Pacific Northwest's "worst mass murder since the Indian wars." Six people were brutally murdered. The seemingly deranged killer used a hammer, black-jack, two kitchen knives, a stove-poker, and a 0.32 caliber revolver in what must have been an hours-long orgy of violence, torture, and death. Luke May, Seattle's famous forensic detective, had to examine an extremely contaminated and chaotic crime scene. The deputy sheriff who guarded the house charged a throng of curious gawkers twenty-five cents each to walk through and get a look before the bodies were finally

Financial scandals over municipal construction projects, such as the Seawall Public Market, helped bring about the end of George Baker's long term as Portland mayor. (*Portland City Archive*)

81

moved. Someone even stole the bloody stockings from the legs of Anna Flieder, one of the victims. May concluded that since Mrs. Flieder's rings (worth $1,400) were missing and the Flieders were known for keeping large sums of cash in the house, the motive must have been robbery, with the six victims killed so they could not identify the thief. May also found blood from an unidentified person in the kitchen. There was evidence that Eugene Chenevert, who had been a professional wrestler, broke through his bonds and fought with the killer before he was battered to death with more than a dozen blows from a hammer.

Details about two of the victims—Anna and Frank Flieder—suggest another motive for the murders. Frank Flieder was a wealthy grocer from Bremerton. His new wife, Anna, was the widow of Bremerton druggist, Clifford Taylor, who had inherited a decent fortune herself. Late in life, the two devoted themselves to pleasure and became notorious for the wild parties they threw at their remote Erland Point home. They were frequently seen gambling for high stakes at Little Dutch's Wigwam, a couple hours' drive away in Olympia. Washington historian Don Moody, in his unpublished 2008 book *The Hammer Murders*, revealed that a week before the murders, the Flieders had traveled to Seattle to arrange licensing for a cabaret and card room they had planned to open. When Anna heard the amount of money that would be needed to "grease" the local organization and receive a license, she hit the roof; in an outburst, she offended a vengeful mobster who put out a contract on her life. Moody's theory seems like a stretch, until you learn the identity of the man Washington eventually executed for the mass murder: Leo Hall.

Hall, who worked in Seattle shipyards before venturing into a life of crime, was a "strong-arm." Strong-arm men earned their living through intimidation. Extortion, badger-games, and armed robbery were typical crimes committed by a strong-arm. In the "badger-game" a strong arm would work with a partner, usually a woman, who would put the victim (known as a mark) into a sexually compromising position. The strong-arm would surprise the couple and extort money from the mark. Hall was an attractive man, a sharp dresser, and he seems to have enjoyed working with female partners. In addition to the usual strong-arm crimes, Hall moonlighted as a contract killer, known as a "button-man."

Hall's role in the Erland Point Massacre was revealed after a failed burglary in Seattle more than eighteen months later. Larry Paulos, a drug-addicted, "habitual criminal" and his partner in crime, Joe Naples, were surprised by the police during the robbery. They escaped in their car after a brief gun battle and fled to Yakima where they were arrested. In the meantime, Seattle police, who knew exactly who they were looking for, went to Paulos' house in Sumner, WA, and arrested his wife, Peggy. Paulos, faced with a life sentence for "assault with a deadly weapon," offered a deal: he would give the prosecutor the men who killed Frank Akin in Portland for a lenient sentence.

Upon his release from the State Penitentiary in Walla Walla, early in 1933, Larry Paulos shared an apartment in downtown Seattle with Leo Hall. Through Hall, Paulos met Jack Justice, who had just moved to Seattle from Portland. Justice, who started out as a chauffeur, was a discreet caterer of vice and influence. Whatever you needed in Portland, Jack was the man to see, fulfilling much the same role as Jake Silverman played in Shy Frank Kodat's organization.[2] Unlike Silverman, though, Justice kept his record fairly clean and had some social prominence; he and his wife were regularly featured in *The Oregonian*'s fashionable society columns. Jack Justice provided connections to a different class of people. One of the services he was able to offer was that of a "fingerman." A fingerman pressed the button that sent a hired killer after a target. Leo Hall was Justice's buttonman. Paulos claimed that first Justice offered him $200 to go to Portland and beat up Frank Akin.

Larry Paulos bungled the job. When Akin found the young ex-convict at his door with a gun in his hand, he punched him in the nose and slammed the door on his wrist, disarming him. Chased from the building by the now-armed Akin, Paulos still grumbled when Justice refused to pay him. Paulos said that was when Justice hired Leo Hall to kill Akin. Paulos said his wife, Peggy, who had been Leo Hall's girlfriend at the time, could corroborate his story.

Peggy Peterson Paulos, still jailed on a bogus charge, grew up in Enumclaw, WA, and had worked as a waitress in restaurants all over Puget Sound. She was a popular waitress and well-known; she had even been to parties at the home of Frank and Anna Flieder. When she heard what Larry had told the police about Leo Hall, she must have been terribly frightened. She knew far worse things about Leo Hall than his involvement in the Akin murder. She had been with him the night of the Erland Point Massacre.

Following the Flieders home from the Wigwam, Peggy thought Hall planned to rob them. It made her nervous that the Flieders might recognize her and Hall promised to blindfold them so they would not see her face. Peggy helped him tie-up the Flieders and their guests: Peggy Chenevert and Magnus Jordan. A few minutes later, Eugene Chenevert and Ezra "Fred" Bolcolm arrived with beer and were then overpowered. Hall took Anna Flieder into the bedroom, where he beat her into unconsciousness and slashed her throat. When Peggy realized that he had murdered Anna Flieder, she ran from the house and Leo fired his pistol at her before turning on the horrified bound witnesses. Peggy ran barefoot through the woods to the house of an acquaintance where she lied to the police on the night of the murder. The crime was not discovered for several days, and by then, everyone had forgotten the terrified, shoeless woman.

Although rumors abounded, Little Dutch was never connected to either crime. Maybe he had nothing to do with it. Maybe it was a coincidence that everyone involved with both murders liked to hang out at the Wigwam. Little Dutch ended up back in prison on a burglary charge in 1935—this time in Walla Walla with his old pals Leo Hall and Frank Butler. He was sentenced to five to fifteen years, but he served almost eight. The last trace of Walter "Little Dutch" Banaster is an arrest in Shasta County, CA, in 1943.

Peggy Paulos' story was enough to convict Leo Hall for the Erland Point Massacre. He was hanged at Walla Walla on September 11, 1936. After Hall's trial, Peggy moved to Portland, where she testified in Jack Justice's trial for the Akin murder. Justice was convicted of manslaughter and got a long sentence in Salem; an occupational hazard for a fingerman. The D.A. emphasized the fact that Justice socialized with Frank Akin and his wife on multiple occasions to suggest he may have had personal motives for killing the man, but everyone believed he had been hired by "higher-ups" to do the job. Justice did his time and steadfastly refused to talk.

8

FAMILY AFFAIRS

[Lover] LaTourell is himself an addict and seems to take fiendish delight in persuading innocent girls to begin the use of the drug [cocaine].

Austin Fiegel, Asst. U.S. Attorney

The white-washed wood-frame building on S.W. 14th Street just off Washington looked like any other building in Portland in 1923, distinguished only by the neatly painted sign above the door: "Fairfield Furnished Rooms by Day, Week or Month." Since her husband, Andrew LaTourell of the famous LaTourell family, died, Clara Penny had been supporting her large family by running a boarding house and brothel. She lost her boarding house license in November 1923, but the brothel remained open. In addition to her young common-law husband, Orville Penny, Clara supported several children: Clarice Irene who was nearly twenty-seven; Andrew Lucian "Lou," twenty-three; Richard "Lover," nineteen; and, Lucille, fourteen. To the Portland Police and *The Oregonian*, they were known as the "notorious LaTourell gang" and also as "half-breed Indians."

Clarice "Clara" Hoover born in 1877 in Texas came to the Pacific Northwest specifically to find a husband. She may have had a previous marriage when she met William Andrew LaTourell in 1893, and he probably seemed like a good catch; after all, there was a waterfall named after him. The Sandy River makes its way to the Columbia by way of several waterfalls that still line a spectacular drive on the Scenic Highway. One of the prettiest falls, just east of Rooster Rock, is named after a colorful early settler who was famous throughout the Pacific Northwest for generosity and hospitality, as well as a good show—William's father, Joseph C. "Frenchy" LaTourell.

Frenchy LaTourell liked to promote the story that he came to Oregon during the Gold Rush in 1845. He even got it into his obituary in *The Oregonian* in 1911, but he admitted in the census of 1900 that he was born in 1837. It was probably quite a bit later when he showed up in Portland at the helm of a river steamboat and began making his living as a "riverman." He tooled a comfortable ride upriver and built a dock and fish-wheel. In 1859, he married Grace Ough, daughter of a prominent Washougal, WA, family. Her father, Richard Augh, was an employee of the Hudson Bay Company

Above left: Richard "Lover" and Honey LaTourell in 1954. They had seen better days when their family was involved in the drug trade. (*Multnomah County Library*)

Above right: Joseph "Frenchy" LaTourell came to Oregon as a young man and started a large family that left its mark on Multnomah County. (*Oregon Historical Society*)

when he arrived at Fort Vancouver in 1809. It was a policy of H.B.C. that factors marry the daughters of important native families. Among the Chinook and Yakama people, it was very difficult to communicate with or trust people who did not have some manner of a family connection. Intermarriage was a common and convenient aid to trading relationships. Grace's mother, Betsie Schleyhoos Augh, was the daughter of an influential native family. Grace, her children, and grandchildren were registered on Yakama tribal rolls for most of their lives.

LaTourell sold his fish in Portland and took visitors on scenic excursions to the romantic falls. Grace, a talented singer and dancer who became famous for her generosity and nursing abilities, provided home-cooked meals and excelled in the domestic arts. Soon, Joseph was a respected river pilot on the tricky stretch between Portland and Cascade Locks and LaTourell Falls was famous for hospitality. In 1871, Joseph petitioned Multnomah County for a road to his "farm," and in 1876, he was appointed postmaster at the Bridal Veil Post Office, which soon changed its name to LaTourell Falls. The LaTourells had a big family: Joseph (1862), Richard (1864), Mason (1865), Alice P. (1867), William Andrew (1871), Clara E. (1875), and Macon B. (1877). Grace taught them all to sing and dance when they were little, and in 1877, regular excursions ran from Portland to see the LaTourell Family perform.

Hard times fell on the children of the pioneers with the Great Depression of 1893, when jobs dried up and money became scarce. You could still feed a family from the natural bounty of the river, though. Joseph and Grace persevered, but the family was touched by scandal in 1895 when Joseph was sued for "alienation of affection" by a neighbor, George Sheppard, in a nasty divorce case involving infidelity. Richard, Frenchy's second son, had ambition as a real estate developer and created the town of Latourell Falls, but soon realized that the nearby town of Troutdale, on the Sandy River provided greener pastures. He and his younger brother, William, known as Andrew, and their sister, Clara Young, a widow with a young son, relocated to Troutdale before 1900. In 1904, Andrew obtained a liquor license from Multnomah County and opened a saloon near Aaron Fox's General Store; by this time, he was married to Clara Hoover, and their children—Irene, Lou, and Lover—were still small.

Aaron Fox was a successful merchant and the postmaster of Troutdale. A settler on the Sandy for twenty years, he had built economic power among the farming communities on the plateau above Latourell Falls. New technology spurred a boom in the area as the price of dried prunes increased as fast as the "high volume" dryers could produce them. The fat safe at Fox's store was a ripe target for robbers from all over and the store regularly lost batches of cash to "yeggs," intent on taking all they could. In 1907, the newly incorporated city elected Fox Troutdale's first mayor. Aaron Fox did not like Indians or "half-breeds" and he did not like saloons. What he did like was a nice quiet town, and he imposed a 9 p.m. curfew, strictly enforced on anyone "underage."

The next few years, Troutdale was a battleground between Aaron Fox and the "saloon interests," represented by Andrew LaTourell and fellow saloonkeeper Charles Rowley. LaTourell ran unsuccessfully for city council in 1908, and Fox's retaliation focused on his opponents' children. In 1909, he arrested sixteen-year-old Charles Rowley, Jr., and fifteen-year-old Irene LaTourell for breaking curfew. Fox took his legal problems to the Multnomah County courts, but his litigious attitude eroded his support in Troutdale; when he bankrupted the city with court fees in an attempt to stop the construction of a new City Hall, that was the end for Aaron Fox. In 1912, women were able to vote legally for the first time in Oregon, and Troutdale elected Clara LaTourell Larrson, now remarried, as the third woman mayor in Oregon.[1]

In December 1912, Troutdale was at the mercy of a gang of thieves, led by Walter Brennan, using the nearby "hobo jungle" as their headquarters. Mayor-elect Larrson's first order of business was to do something about the "terror gang." On December 13, two weeks before the new mayor was to take office, Brennan and his gang surrounded her house, terrorizing her family. Clara held Brennan at gunpoint for several hours before the police finally arrived and hauled him off to jail. Clara saved the small city from the predators, but it was not long before her brother's teenage children became the main problem.

Irene, the oldest, had been running with a fast and dangerous crowd, which included Allen Tanner, a teenage burglar and car thief, and Al Ilog, a young mechanic who liked to drive too fast. In 1917, sixteen-year-old Lover was arrested with Tanner in a stolen car. The arrest alerted police to a gang of car thieves that were burglarizing stores in suburbs all around Portland. A few months later, when the gang hit Aaron Fox's store in Troutdale, the police swooped in arresting Tanner, Lucian LaTourell (eighteen), and his brother, Lover, along with a couple of other teenagers. Lover escaped to Portland, dying his hair bright red and hiding from the police for nearly a year to avoid a sentence in the state reformatory at Woodburn. Lucian was sentenced to a year in county jail.

Andrew LaTourell died in 1918 and his wife, Clara, moved with their children to Portland. She was estranged from the extended LaTourell family after the death of her husband, partly because of the embarrassing legal troubles her children faced, but also because of her penchant for young lovers and her heavy use of alcohol and drugs. In 1920, Clara opened the Fairfield Rooms in Portland. By then, Lucian and Lover had become the city's most reliable suppliers of cocaine and morphine and the new "rooming house" soon became the site of a series of "coke parties" that were held responsible for destroying the morals of some of Portland's teenage girls. Irene married Al Ilog after he returned from military service in World War I. She ran the day-to-day business of the Fairfield Rooms for her mother and the Ilog Inn, her husband's roadhouse near Gresham, became a "chop shop" for stolen cars.

Portland did not like "half-breeds" any better than Troutdale had, especially when they ran wild the way Lucian and Lover LaTourell did. Dozens of arrests followed as the boys became the Portland police bureau's definition of the "usual suspects." Occasionally, they were arrested with small amounts of drugs or burglar tools on them, but usually the police had to settle for a charge of simple vagrancy. The two brothers made regular appearances at police court and served numerous sentences in the city jail, usually thirty days or less. Much of their profit from illegal activity went to lawyer fees during this time.

The police bureau took the unusual step of stationing an officer at the door of the notorious Fairfield Rooms to discourage their business. (*Multnomah County Library*)

In 1920, Lucian and Lover met two sisters from Dufur, OR, on the Columbia River, Josephine and Hazel Lewis. Lucian married Josephine in 1920 and Richard married Hazel a few years later. Hazel, under the name Hazel Edwards, and Josephine LaTourell became as notorious as the LaTourell brothers, making frequent appearances in police court and serving several short sentences in jail or at the Cedars Detention Hospital for Women on the all-purpose charge of vagrancy. In August 1920, Portland recognized that cocaine had become a serious problem when the City Messenger Service was raided, and four young messenger boys were arrested for a drug delivery plot. Lucian LaTourell was arrested at the same time and his wild "coke parties" became common knowledge. *The Oregonian* wrung its hands at all the young ladies from "respectable families" who were using cocaine and morphine and Lucian went back to the County Jail for six months.

In 1923, the troubles of the LaTourells finally came to a head. First Irene's marriage to Al Ilog broke down in a series of loud, violent quarrels that may have been Irene's cries for help. She served several short jail terms for public disturbances and Al ended up in the state penitentiary for two years on a stolen car charge. That did not stop Irene who was arrested a dozen times in 1922 and 1923. In October, she was picked up after a loud temper tantrum over a broken-down car. The problem was that her car had stalled on Southeast Stark Street near 29th, in what was considered a respectable neighborhood. The case brought an interesting acknowledgement from *The Oregonian*: "The north end or the south end or upper Washington Street may be a lawful habitat for the underworld."

Irene, emotional and uncontrollable, may have spilled the beans on her family's activities. Shortly after Irene's arrest, Clara Penny lost her boarding house license, and a couple of weeks later, the police raided the Fairfield Rooms, arresting Clara and both of her sons, along with several other people. *The Oregonian* noted that in the last fifteen months, there had been twenty-six arrests at the Fairfield for various vice, liquor, and narcotics violations. The next day, the police bureau took the unusual action of stationing a police officer at the door of the Fairfield to look menacing and discourage its clientele. It may be the first time the Portland police tried to coerce someone out of business with this tactic, but it would not be the last.

Police harassment created real hardship for the family business. Heavy legal fees tied up the LaTourells' funds; at one point, the family had $1,100 (more than $16,000 today) posted as bonds for various family members facing legal charges. Hostility from the police department made it difficult for the family to obtain illegal liquor, and their business depended more and more on acquiring and distributing illegal drugs. Lover, who was caught with cocaine during the Fairfield raid, spent seventy-five days in jail and then started spending time in San Francisco, where he eventually stayed for more than a decade. Lucian was arrested more than a dozen times over the next few years, but never stayed in jail long. The cases against him often fell apart due to lack of evidence. Lucian had domestic problems of his own, though. His marriage to Josephine did not survive the 1920s and soon dissolved.

Clara Penny, with a police officer stationed at her door twenty-four-hours a day, had to close the Fairfield. She continued to operate her business but moving from location to location took a toll on her, and she was not able to earn a living. In 1928, along with her new lover and future husband, Ash Fellows, and her daughter, Lucille (now nineteen), Clara was arrested for shoplifting at Olds, Wortman and King Department Store. A search of Clara's apartment found four suitcases full of stolen silk undergarments worth about $2,000. Fellows was sentenced to a year at hard labor at the Kelly Butte rock pile. Clara and Lucille were given a choice—six months in county jail or exile from Multnomah County for that time.

In the first two months of 1928, Portland became very excited over a criminal called the "Blonde Burglar." She committed burglaries all over the east side, often calling her victim first to make sure the house was empty and sometimes leaving taunting notes behind. The main suspect for these crimes turned out to be Frankie Willis, real name Frances Weller. She provided an alibi; she was in Klamath Falls in January and February when the Blonde Burglar was most active, but she was certainly committing burglaries with her lover, Lucian LaTourell, and the stigma of the Blonde Burglar followed her for years.[2] Over the next four years, Lucian and Frances became familiar to readers of *The Oregonian* as they were charged with a series of Portland burglaries. They were married in 1930, and evidence points to the fact that they spent a lot of time in Klamath Falls, where they may have been fencing stolen goods from both Portland and San Francisco.

The Oregonian never reported the name of Lucian LaTourell's attorney, but he did an excellent job of keeping his client out of jail. Facing dozens of charges in several court appearances in both Oregon and California, Lucian never spent much time in jail. Frances Weller was not so lucky; in June 1928, at the age of twenty-two, she was sentenced to eighteen months in the State Industrial School for Women on a state vagrancy charge. When she was released, Weller became much better at discretion and managed to avoid the police, although she was wanted on burglary charges, until February 1932. On the evening of February 10, Lucian entered the home of R. B. Runyon at the Santa Barbara Apartments on southeast Hawthorne Street. Mrs. Runyon, who had left the building only moments before, saw the light come on in her window and went back. With the help of a neighbor, Mrs. Runyon found Lucian hiding in a closet and held him until the police arrived.[3]

Caught red-handed, Lucian was held in the city jail. Frances and Lucian's mother, now Clara Fellows, were arrested when they came to pay his $5,000 bail. Frances was wanted for another burglary in December of a southeast Portland apartment and she was carrying narcotics in her purse when she arrived at the police station. Mrs. Fellows was "held for the district attorney." When the Fellows' apartment on northeast Fremont Street was searched, police discovered thousands of dollars' worth of stolen clothing, jewelry, and radios. Oddly, Clara did not face any charges in the case. Frances and Lucian were indicted for multiple burglaries and faced federal narcotics charges. Things looked bad for the LaTourells, but Lucian's sudden death at the age of thirty-two from a "liver disease" on March 15, cleared things up. It seems likely he was suffering from severe drug addiction.[4] Frances still faced burglary charges, but *The Oregonian* never reported the outcome of her case, and in a few years, she settled down in N.W. Portland, a well-to-do widow.

Lucian LaTourell may have been the most famous member of the black sheep branch of his family, but Honey LaTourell, whoever she was, was a strong competitor. Evidence points to Lucian's youngest sister, Lucille, as Honey, but a death notice in *The Oregonian* claims Lucille died in 1946 at the age of thirty-seven. Two other women could have been Honey LaTourell, Hazel Lewis, Richard's wife, born in 1901 or Vivian Owens, Irene's daughter, born in 1914. Based on her age, Owens is the most likely suspect.

Who was Honey LaTourell? Using various names, Marion Forrest and Maxine Burns among them, Honey became involved with a drug-smuggling ring being run by members of the Kung Bow Leong Chinese Tong, selling a new product that was gaining in popularity—heroin. Her partner was Eddie Wong, a Chinese-American man born in San Francisco who began his career before World War I as a "hatchetman" for the Tong.

Tacit agreement between the racist city of Portland and the powerful minority group commonly referred to as Chinatown or "celestials," provided a unique situation for Chinese and Chinese-American Portlanders. Since the beginning of Portland's history in the 1850s, Chinese people made up about one-quarter of the city's population. Wealthy citizens relied on the Chinese as domestic servants, kitchen and of course laundry workers. The labor-intensive industries of Oregon relied on a large group of transient workers, many of them Chinese, most of whom spent the rainy season in Portland. Chinatown's population often tripled in the winter. Officially, Chinatown was treated as a separate entity and Chinese citizens rarely cooperated with authorities. The police left the Chinese to themselves, often even refusing to investigate murders, as in the 1892 case of Gong Fa, which I describe in my book *Murder and Mayhem in Portland*. Violent conflict over economic issues was common in Chinatown, and the "tongs" grew as protective organizations and benevolent societies. Most of the tongs were never involved in illegal activities, but they all enforced strict discipline among their members and defended themselves from hostile white people and other tongs with armed toughs known as hatchetmen.

Portland police treated Chinatown as a separate world where the Hop Sing Tong eventually gained control of vice. (*Portland Police Historical Society*)

It is difficult to obtain information on the tongs in Portland. Not only must the researcher be fluent in Chinese, but even then, they must overcome the strong rule of silence that was violently enforced in the nineteenth and twentieth centuries. In addition, the trope of "tong war" has been used so often to inflame racial hatred that any reporting in the press is suspect. Police records are no better. Few Portland police spoke Chinese, and the few Chinese witnesses who did cooperate were often conmen or criminals, like Eddie Wong. We do know that there were several episodes of shocking violence and murder in Chinatown, and they seemed to center around a conflict between the Kung Bow Leong and Hop Sing tongs who fought over gambling and drugs.

Eddie Wong was rounded up in a group of "usual suspects" after a "tong war" incident in 1917, but charges were dropped for lack of evidence. In 1918, he wrote a letter to District Attorney Walter Evans from "somewhere in France" where he was serving with Battery "B" of the 65th Artillery. According to *The Oregonian*, "Wong wrote an especially optimistic letter, giving high praise for the abundant food and clothing with which the United States troops are provided and confidently predicting that his next letter would be mailed in Berlin." It seems Eddie was a bit of a smart-ass, which is probably why Honey liked him. Eddie and Honey were arrested together by federal narcotics agents, and they faced charges together more than once in the mid-1930s as Honey set up the distribution system for the heroin import/export clerk, Eddie, was bringing into Portland.

In 1940, sixty-three-year-old Clara Fellows, a widow for the second time, purchased an old brick building on the southwest corner of Burnside and Third Avenue, a building that now houses Dante's Nightclub. Lover, her son Richard now almost forty, returned from San Francisco to manage what was then called the Hotel Clare. Lover's wife, Hazel, ran the brothel. Irene, forty-six, took over housekeeping, now using the name Cleries Davis. Honey worked as desk clerk in the small lobby. With Honey's drug connections, the Hotel Clare and Burke's Café, directly across Burnside Street, became the city's central distribution point for heroin as its popularity took off. Clara must have found some kind of protection because although the Hotel Clare faced the usual raids, serious charges were never brought against any of the LaTourells during this time.

Honey LaTourell became a well-known character in the bar scene in the North End. The notorious Jim Elkins had several bars and after-hours clubs in the neighborhood, and he liked to put old boxers "out to pasture" in their own place. Chuck Brown, an African American ex-boxer, entertained his customers with tall tales at a bar he operated right around the corner from Burke's Café. Nick De Pinto, one of Bobby Evan's enforcers who spent more than a decade in prison, had a bar just blocks away. The Cecil Rooms, run by ex-boxer Pat O'Day, notorious for the murder of Capt. Frank Tatum (a story I tell in detail in *Portland on the Take*) was a few blocks south. Even Jack Justice's bar, the Santa Fe, infamous from the 1930s Akin Case, was within walking distance of the Hotel Clare. Three blocks west on Burnside was the Follies, where "Torrid Terry" Lane, the redheaded bombshell, and Betty Ann Wade, the Cocktail Girl, performed regularly.

The people who frequented these drinking establishments were as interesting and colorful as the proprietors. You had to bring your own bottle because it was illegal to buy liquor by the glass, but a "night on the town" was the thing to do, and Portlanders from all walks of life came to rub elbows with the underworld and the underworld rubbed back. Harold "Hal" Seahorn worked here and there as a bouncer, but his main

The Hotel Clare, on the south side of Burnside, and Burke's Café, visible in the center of the picture, became the focal point of heroin distribution in the 1940s. (*Portland City Archive*)

racket was the badger game with his "wife," photographer Shirley Higdon. "Stormy Jean" Duncan, related to the Duncan criminal family of North Portland, which was involved in several murders, hung out in the bars in the neighborhood.[5] She was a recruiter for her brothers' prostitution ring, but her specialty was actually rolling drunks for their wallets. Phyllis "Torchy" Jessing, a flame-haired barmaid, got her start in the neighborhood as well. Torchy made a name for herself in 1958 when she stabbed her boyfriend. Her initials on the knife she used gave her away at her assault trial.

In addition to slumming Portlanders and the underworld figures who preyed on them, the neighborhood of the Hotel Clare was a place for drug-addicts, such as Lee Butler, an ex-special policeman who played accordion, and Jimmy Valentine, a card dealer, to hang out. Sailors, like Roman Podlas and Pierre Schultz, frequented the neighborhood, which also was the home of the Sailor's Union.[6] Countless misguided teenagers like Joann Dewey and her friend Joan Crawford also hung out there. Honey LaTourell, whoever she was, fit right in with these characters.

The 1940s was not a bad decade for the LaTourells, but things got worse after Clara Fellows passed away at the age of seventy-two in 1949. Her protection held for a short time; when Irene was found dead in her room just a month after her mother died, her death was never investigated. Clara's protection did not last, and Lover and Honey were arrested several times for petty crimes starting in 1950. Even worse, Eddie Wong died that same year and Honey lost her heroin connection as the Hop Sing Tong consolidated its hold on Portland's heroin trade. In November 1950, after a couple of

Lorali "The Girl with Million Dollar Legs" performed at the Star Theater not far from the Hotel Clare. (*Oregon Historical Society*)

violent incidents at the Hotel Clare, Lover sold the building at the fire-sale price of $700 (about $7,000 today).

In 1952, Richard was sentenced to the state penitentiary for two years on a charge of receiving stolen property. By that time, his addiction to heroin was quite advanced and he received little help for his problem in prison. Honey was using heroin heavily as well and was arrested more than once for solicitation; *The Oregonian* usually remarked on her illness from drug withdrawal. She found a job running a transient hotel on S.W. 1st Avenue in the heart of Portland's Tenderloin district and moved in with her new lover, Jimmie Valentine. When Lover was released from the state penitentiary, he moved into the building where Honey lived. In 1954, the last act of the LaTourells sordid story played out.

On March 19, a desperate gunman pushed his way into the luxurious West Hills home of George Brice, Jr., a wealthy realtor/real estate developer. Confronting Mrs. Brice and her maid, Lizzie Brown, with a pistol, the gunman demanded they turn over Buck Brice, the family's eight-year-old son, whom he would release in return for a ransom of $125,000. On learning that Buck was in class at the exclusive Catlin-Hillside School, the gunman forced the two women into their car and made them drive to the school. When they arrived, Mrs. Brice told the principal to call the police and two of the teachers fought the gunman. After firing a couple of shots, wounding one of the teachers and terrorizing a fifth-grade classroom, the gunman fled, his absurd kidnapping plot comically foiled.

The case received a great deal of attention. Under intense pressure to find the kidnapper, the Portland police conducted "the biggest dragnet in Pacific Northwest history." A few days after the kidnapping, "secret information" led detectives to the rooming house on S.W. 1st Avenue where they found and arrested Jimmie Valentine, who looked a little like drawings of the suspect, along with Honey and Lover LaTourell. No one thought the LaTourell's were involved in the kidnapping. Yet they were still both arrested for "vagrancy by drug addiction." Apparently, they were both highly intoxicated on heroin when the police arrived. According to *The Oregonian*, Jimmie Valentine "appeared to be suffering from the inner fires of withdrawal of narcotics."

What followed next was a show trial that gave Portlanders one of their first exposures to heroin addicts and the sordid drama that often illuminates their dark world. Evidence was inconclusive and Valentine was acquitted of the kidnapping. As usual in cases like this, the police dropped the investigation when their suspect was acquitted and no one ever found out who tried to kidnap the Brice boy, if anyone did. Further investigation of the case shows that George Brice, Jr., was involved with running a prostitution operation, the Loma Rooms, out of his real estate office and may have been behind in his protection payments. The "kidnapping" could have been a way to put pressure on him to make a payment. The case has the fingerprints of "vice king" Jim Elkins all over it.

The case further provided Honey LaTourell with a brief moment of local fame as she was an important witness, backing up Valentine's alibi. It was about the end for the LaTourell gang, though. Honey moved to Sherwood, OR, far out of town and only made brief visits to Portland, including a spectacular jailbreak, following a vagrancy arrest in 1958. Richard "Lover" lived the next few years in transient hotels in the Tenderloin district with occasional arrests for vagrancy, shoplifting, or other petty crimes until his death in 1971.

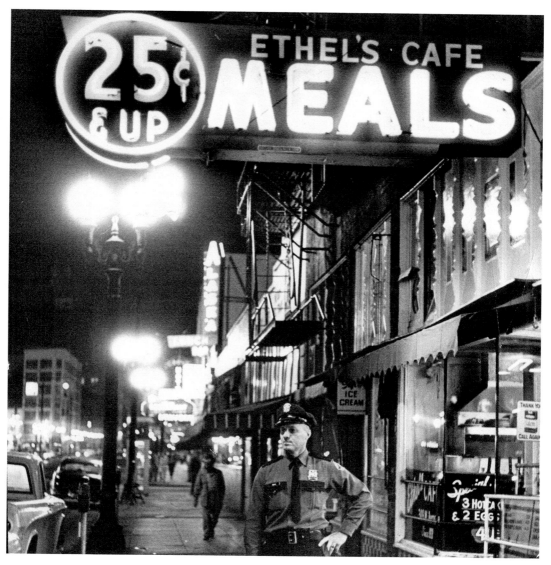

Burke's Café changed its name to Ethel's in the 1950s and was featured in this classic photograph of Officer Fred Wallo taken by Alan Delay. (*Portland Police Historical Society*)

9

Separate but Equal

Money is power.

Tom Johnson

"Nothing before 1916 had anything on the green two-storied shanty at 535 Savier Street," *The Oregonian* gushed on August 31, 1932. The front-page story, under the headline "1932 Model Saloon Portland's Latest," lovingly described the luxurious saloon in what amounted to a front-page ad for the illegal business where "rye, bourbon, gin, beer and champagne were on tap and available from twenty-five to sixty-five cents a drink." It reported that the swanky place had been "taken down" on August 17 but made sure its readers knew that it was open that night.

The Greenfront Saloon, as it was known at the time, was a model of what Portland could provide with legal drinking and gambling. By 1932, most Americans were ready to admit that Prohibition had been a mistake and the repeal of the 18th Amendment was well underway. The current slogan was, "Beer by Christmas." At the Greenfront, a shot of whisky or gin or a big schooner of beer was a quarter. White Rock highballs were available for fifty cents, and celebrants could also have champagne for sixty-five cents a glass. Excellent food (their specialty was chicken dinner) was available from a clean kitchen and served by waiters in starched white jackets. The blackjack table was busy. "An excellent blues singer and a gifted piano player whiled away the passing hours," *The Oregonian* reported, "Negroes attended to all the service while other Negroes appeared to be in positions of authority."

The one thing *The Oregonian* did not mention was the name of the man who owned the place: Tom Johnson. He was a big man, standing 6 feet 2 inches and weighing in at 220 pounds. He had an imposing physical presence, but a quiet demeanor. In his fifteen years since returning from the fighting frontlines of France, Mr. Johnson (as he was widely known) had risen to be the undisputed leader of Portland's small, tightly-connected African American community. Robert Dietsche, in *Jumptown: The Golden Years of Portland Jazz 1942–1957*, gives us the most vivid portrait yet of the man and the empire he built, especially his crowning achievement: The Avenue.

Over a long career, Tom Johnson (left) became the undisputed leader of Portland's African American community. (*Urban League of Portland Records (MSS UrbanLeague), Oregon State University Special Collections and Archives Research Center, Corvallis, Oregon*)

Bill McLendon, publisher of *The Portland Observer* newspaper and a jazz pianist, explained his long relationship with Tom Johnson to Robert Dietsche:

> In his mind vice could be virtue. You take from the more-than-willing customers. You give a little to City Hall. You invest the rest and give some of it back to the community in loans. You employ hundreds of people and you get to play jazz all night.

In 1932, Johnson's ideal was under attack as he was embroiled in the fight of his life with the white power structure, which held all of Portland in its tight fist.

Born in Louisiana in 1888, Johnson's parents were plantation slaves until June 19, 1865, when the black people of Texas were freed. The Johnson family lived in fear of the race-based system of terror imposed by white vigilantes after the Reconstruction Era collapsed in 1876. When their older brother was murdered by the Ku Klux Klan, teenage Tom and his younger brother, William, went north looking for jobs. They found them with the Southern Pacific Railroad in Kansas City shortly after the turn of the twentieth century.

Johnson worked as a gandy-dancer, doing the hardest labor on the track maintenance crew. He grew from a gangly teenager into a muscular young man as he rode the rails regularly from Kansas City to Oakland and then to Portland. He had a good sense of

Pullman porters had to put up with a lot on their job, but they brought African American culture and new music to an entertainment-starved country. (*Oregon Historical Society*)

humor, a quick mind, and he loved music. He made friends easily with the numerous Pullman porters who worked the passenger cars, many of whom were also musicians.

Frederick Douglass had been a U.S. marshal, and occasionally, there was an African American member of Congress, but in the early twentieth century, working as a Pullman porter was the most prestigious job a black man could realistically hope to attain. A growing number of black doctors, lawyers, and businessmen were making their mark, but the porters were the coolest of the cool, bringing the latest black culture and music to a country starving for entertainment. Some of them saw themselves as ambassadors to a benighted world. As Wynton Marsalis explained in the film *Ken Burn's Jazz*, "Accepting the music meant accepting the humanity of the Negro."

Uniformly called "George" by patronizing and often abusive passengers, the porters rode the trains to take care of everything and they had to put up with a lot. They performed the most distasteful jobs with cool smiles. It would be decades before their secret organization would emerge as the Brotherhood of Sleeping Car Porters, and under the leadership of A. Philip Randolph, it would become one of the most important labor organizations in American history. Even so, the brotherhood always existed among these men. They knew how to keep secrets, and they knew why they should keep them.

Most of the men who worked with Tom Johnson in the early years had been porters, and many of them were musicians as well. That was probably what attracted Mr. Johnson to them in the first place. He was a passionate man who loved music, horses, and pretty, young women, and he wanted the money it would take to indulge those passions regularly. Fortunately, he had a knack for making money, and when he settled in Portland in 1910, he had enough to buy a small parcel of land.

Legends about Mr. Johnson, which grew around him like a fogbank, said the money came from the Humboldt bullion robbery, but in a career that skirted the law for six decades, during which he was arrested more than fifty times, Johnson never spent a night in jail. Wherever the money came from, he used it to buy a large lot on N.W. Savier Street between Fifteenth and Sixteenth. It was a bit outside the boundary of Darktown, where black people were allowed to live mostly without harassment, but everybody knew that the few blocks near Union Depot were bursting at the seams and Darktown would have to expand. Mr. Johnson's place would first be the nucleus of an expanding black community and eventually, as Tom Johnson's Chicken Dinner Inn, would become a nationally known Portland landmark.

It was not much in 1910—not more than a shack on a big lot. It became the Orpheus Club, the private club and playground for the Pullman porters. It was a comfortable place where the porters could relax, have a drink, smoke a little something, tell stories, and play jazz. Twenty-two-year-old Tom Johnson was the boss and he was done with manual labor. He began wearing his trademark brown western-cut suit and Stetson hat and he joined the town's merchant community, as much as Portland would let a black man join.

Portland was the largest city in a state founded as a "white man's paradise" where people of color were to be excluded. That deluded dream died quickly, and most Portlanders felt it was not fair to discriminate against a man because of the color of his skin, but they looked on non-white people as somehow different and not quite as good as the white population.

The Indians, who were devastated by starvation, war, and disease, provided steady labor, especially in factory jobs. The Chinese, who always made up at least one-quarter of the city's population, were indispensable as a reliable source of labor. The tiny African American community, numbering only a few hundred members, was important to the service industry, making up a large percentage of the city's food and beverage servers, porters, and janitors. The city soon learned to neglect the minority communities as long as they were quiet. If any conflict got too loud, then it quickly became a police problem. Chinatown, Darktown, and Little Tokyo became separate, isolated worlds that white people only visited to "kick the gong around" and amuse themselves. Mr. Johnson, who was famous for ordering enormous Chinese meals at the New Republic Café on Northwest Fourth, must have admired the discipline the tongs enforced and the wealth the Chinese merchants were able to reap from their large labor force.[1]

As an old man, years later, Johnson had a particular phrase he always said when pressing a silver dollar into his granddaughter's hand: "Money is power." He learned that lesson early and he had a good teacher. Walter A. "Emanuel" Green was a prospector who joined the Colorado gold rush at the age of thirteen in 1878. He was not only the youngest mine owner in Cripple Creek, but he was also the first black man to stake a mining claim there. In 1899, he arrived in Portland with enough money to open a real estate office and start offering mining opportunities for sale. His light skin helped Green "pass" for white when necessary, and by 1910, when he met Tom Johnson, he was a respected realtor, moving easily in both black and white Portland. He taught Johnson what to do with his money and inspired another regular phrase Mr. Johnson used often, "If you have money, buy real estate."

The Golden West Hotel was the only place for African-American visitors to stay in Portland. Its penthouse suites were the home of the bootleggers who operated the Pullman Porters Ring. (*Oregon Historical Society*)

In the second decade of the twentieth century, young black musicians were turning the musical world on its ear as they created the vital music that would become both jazz and blues. The Golden West Hotel is credited with Portland's first jazz performance in 1914, but by then, the jam sessions at the Orpheus Club had been going on for years. By 1916, when alcohol became illegal in Oregon, the Orpheus had relaxed its membership rules and become a popular musical club. There is no evidence that Johnson was involved in organized bootlegging before his military service, but you could always get a drink at the Orpheus Club with Johnson in charge.

When Prohibition began in Oregon, the Pullman porters on the Southern Pacific between Oakland and Portland were faced with intense demand for liquor from their passengers. Always willing to please, the porters invented several unique ways to meet the demand. One notable invention was the hand-flask—flasks the size of silver dollars that held about four tablespoons of whisky and sold for fifty cents. With liquor still legal in California, the SP trains had booze to spare, and the porters were glad to share with thirsty Portland. Originally organized by white Oregon businessmen working with two San Francisco distilleries, the Pullman porter bootlegging ring became the most consistent source of alcohol in dry Oregon.

Tom Johnson was drafted in 1917 and served on the frontlines in France, where many all-black units saw heavy fighting and casualties. He was back in Portland in 1919 and working for Sam "Yam" Wallace, who was operating the porters' ring by that time. Wallace and his sidekick, John Lowe, had taken control of the liquor when the original white organizers of the bootlegging ring were arrested in a large raid in 1918.[2] John Lowe, a violent man who excelled at armed robbery, had a strong relationship with police Captain Harry Circle, ironically the highest-ranking Portland officer to join the Ku Klux Klan. Lowe's relationship with Circle provided valuable protection from the police. Wallace drove a flashy car and strutted through the lobby of the Golden West Hotel, where he lived in a penthouse. He liked to call himself the "King of Darktown."

Mr. Johnson went to work for Yam Wallace when he got back from the war and continued to run the Porter's Club in his old place. At this point in his career, Johnson was more commonly known as "Nigger Tom." He learned the basics of bootlegging and was known for his creative methods of hiding booze in unusual places. In one memorable case in 1920, Johnson was arrested wearing an overcoat that had 12 pints of whisky hanging on strings inside it.

When Wallace and Lowe had a falling out in 1920, Lowe was kicked out of the liquor ring. Johnson saw an opportunity to seize control of the lucrative business and he made his move. When three out-of-town tough guys confronted Yam Wallace at the Golden West Hotel, he ran from them and was humiliated. Was it merely coincidence that the tough guys came from Kansas City, where Tom Johnson had friends? Johnson spread malicious rumors about the humiliated crime boss, and when Wallace confronted him, they fought. Johnson, who carried a straight razor for protection, cut Wallace badly, as *The Oregonian* reported "in the region where the parental razor strop is frequently employed."

Yam Wallace threatened to kill Johnson and the police arrested him, in his hospital bed, for issuing threats. After Wallace was released on bail, he was caught with $10,000 worth of cocaine in his possession and went away for a long stretch at McNeil Island Federal Penitentiary. For the next four decades, bad things just seemed to happen to

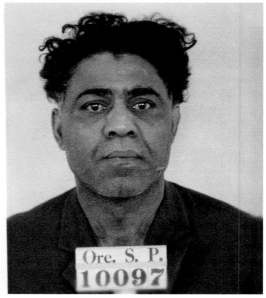

John Lowe, enraged by his exclusion from the Porters Ring, took his revenge with armed robbery. He ended up in prison, where he died in 1930. (*Oregon State Archive*)

people who opposed the legendary Tom Johnson. Police Chief Leon Jenkins had been a Darktown police officer in 1910, when Johnson arrived in town. The two men had known each other for a decade in 1920. The extent of the relationship between Johnson and Jenkins cannot be proved, but evidence indicates they were close. Making a deal with Jenkins to keep Darktown peaceful, Johnson not only gained control of the liquor coming in on the Southern Pacific, but he also became the undisputed leader of Darktown with the chief's tacit support. Fifty years after the big man's death, Johnson was still remembered in Albina as a man who was both loved and feared.

Mr. Johnson beat two federal indictments for violating the National Prohibition Act. First, he was acquitted in Seattle in 1927; then, charges were dropped in Chicago in 1930 after a Pullman porter, Rudolph Young, took the rap and went to jail. By 1932, Johnson bragged that he was untouchable in Portland and that the Feds could not get him. His bravado notwithstanding, Tom Johnson was on shakier ground than he may have realized. Things started to go bad in October 1930 when a Portland police officer with a reputation for brutality was found mysteriously dead on property owned by Mr. Johnson.

About 8 a.m. Saturday, October 11, 1930, Robert Drake, a veteran patrolman on "the toughest beat in town," was found dying in the basement of the Automobile Finance Company at the corner of Northwest Broadway and Couch in Darktown. Johnson owned the used car dealership and often used it as a temporary speakeasy during large events, like the Shriners' Conventions that regularly came to town. Drake was found on a pile of scrap wood about 15 feet from the bottom of a short elevator shaft that opened onto the street near a police callbox. His back was broken, and he had several injuries that might have come from a fall down the shaft. Drake died at St. Vincent's Hospital later that morning.

According to *The Oregonian,* "the detective division was inclined to dismiss the death as accidental." Dr. W. C. Hunter of the University of Oregon, who performed the *post-mortem* for the coroner's office, found an odd discrepancy, though: Drake had been struck on the temporal bone by a blunt object. It looked like an injury from the leather sap that all officers carried (Drake's sap was found at the bottom of the shaft), and the bruise could not be accounted for by the fall. Dr. Hunter thought the bruise indicated that Drake was knocked unconscious and then thrown down the shaft. Oddly enough, Drake's cap was still tight on his head when he was found, snugly covering a severe head wound. How someone with a fractured skull and broken spine could walk the 15 feet from the elevator shaft to where the body was found was unexplained.

The coroner ruled the death accidental and decided no inquest was necessary, but outcry from Drake's family and friends raised difficult questions and the coroner was forced to reverse the decision. An inquest was held ten days after Drake's mysterious death. Witnesses told conflicting stories; many of them complained about police harassing them and they changed their stories more than once. Drake's partner, Ales Lander, another veteran patrolman with a reputation for brutality, took the stand and gave what some considered a humorous performance, describing how he and Drake had almost fallen down that same shaft on a previous occasion. Drake, he said, had laughed, saying, "It would be a fine mess for them to find a couple of bulls all piled up down there in the morning." The jury ruled Drake's death an accident and it was added to the long list of mysterious deaths making headlines in the early 1930s, which often defied logic and common sense.

When a rival bootlegger, Tom Henderson, tried to muscle him at his home, in an effort at intimidation, in March 1931, Johnson had him arrested for issuing threats while armed with a gun. Henderson claimed that he had not been armed and that the gun actually belonged to Johnson, but the police did not believe him. Even with Johnson's strong relationship with the police, he was feeling the pressure. A few days after that incident, one of Mr. Johnson's enforcers, Sam Shelby, shot Harry Vessel at the Porter's Club, which by then had relocated to Williams Avenue on the east side. Vessel would be a thorn in Mr. Johnson's side for at least a decade as he tried to muscle in on his business, but it was clear that Johnson's agreement to keep the peace in Darktown was getting more difficult to accomplish.

Federal Agent Wayne E. Kain, a 1917 graduate of Washington High School, began to increase the pressure on Johnson in 1931, raiding several of his places over the summer. Johnson was still relying on the Pullman porters to bring in bonded liquor from Canada, but he had begun to manufacture his own beer and whiskey at a large distillery and brewery located on North Vancouver Avenue. Next door to the brewery was a house that served as the distribution center for his narcotics operation, at that time focusing mostly on marijuana (known as muggles or tea) and cocaine. Johnson's wife, Mary, became a licensed real estate agent by 1930, and she and Emanuel Green bought property all over town, especially focusing on busy Williams, Vancouver, and Mississippi Avenues in North Portland. Eventually, with Mary's help, Johnson owned well over one hundred separate properties. As housing segregation became more and more entrenched these neighborhoods became the site of an expanded black community,

Horace and George Duke (front row third and fourth from the left) were the only black police officers in Portland until the 1950s. (*Portland Police Historical Society*)

which was slowly relocating from the old Darktown locations of the past. As if staking a claim for the future, Johnson purchased a house on Northeast 28th Street in the 1920s, and by the end of Mr. Johnson's career in the 1960s, North and Northeast Portland would be considered "the Ghetto."

Although it was always legal for people of any race to own property anywhere in Portland, housing segregation was a reality. A 1919 amendment to the Realtor's Code made it an ethical violation to sell real estate to black or Asian buyers in predominantly white neighborhoods. A good example of how neighborhoods reacted to black families buying property is the collective reaction of the Westmoreland neighborhood when Dr. DeNorval Unthank purchased a house on southeast Knapp Avenue in April 1931.

Over a long career, Dr. Unthank became Oregon's most important African American physician and has a park named for him in the Albina neighborhood. When he and his young family (his wife, Thelma, and their twenty-one-month-old daughter) moved into their new home, they found nearly every window had been broken. Angry white neighbors mobbed the sidewalk in front of their house, protesting a black family in the neighborhood. A few days later, an elected committee visited the doctor with an offer to buy his property at a good profit, if the family would move.

Dr. Unthank refused the committee's offer and tensions rose through May and June. After another round of window-breaking, tensions came to a head on June 28, 1931.

The young son of the Unthanks' next-door neighbors, Mr. and Mrs. Fred James, told the Unthanks that his father bragged about breaking the windows. When Dr. Unthank and his wife, Thelma, confronted the white couple next door, an argument between the two wives turned into a near brawl. Thelma allegedly said, "I have a gun and I shoot straight." She was arrested and charged with issuing threats.

The Unthanks complained that the police refused to provide protection for them as crowds of as many as fifty angry people mobbed the sidewalk in front of their home through May and June, loudly complaining and disturbing the peace. As the unofficial leader of Darktown, Tom Johnson saw himself as the protector of the black community and often used his influence to help settle disputes. Taking advantage of his close relationship with Police Chief Jenkins, Johnson negotiated a deal with the police to allow him to protect the Unthanks: as long as no one carried firearms, the police would ignore any armed black people who happened to be around the Unthank home. Sam Shelby, who consistently worked as a strong-arm enforcer for Mr. Johnson, was probably one of the men, rumored to carry baseball bats, who kept the sidewalks clear around the doctor's house. After Mrs. Unthank's arrest, an agreement was made with the neighborhood committee and charges were dropped. The Unthanks kept their home, for a while; eventually, their growing family moved to a larger home in northeast Portland.

Tom Johnson exploited the working class of his neighborhood and enriched himself by promoting their addictions to alcohol, drugs, gambling, and sex. He used his riches to buy important properties that he could turn into massive profit from lucrative government deals, which eventually destroyed the vital community he had helped build. He learned to play the white man's game so well he could almost pass, if he was not so black.

Tom Johnson was a complex and often contradictory character. Even with his faults, Johnson did important things for his community. Through profiteering and promoting addiction, Johnson's business interests destroyed numerous families, but as much as he destroyed it, Johnson in many ways was responsible for the growth of that vital community. He led the way in moving "his people" —the black railroad and service industry workers who doubled as businessmen, scientists, artists, journalists and such— from the cramped corner of Chinatown known as Darktown to "the other side."

In 1930, Portland had one of the most highly educated and literate working classes in the country. Nowhere else were you more likely to get a shoeshine from a black man with a master's degree than in Portland. They wanted to start families and own businesses, but the neighborhood they were confined to was the most dangerous and exploitive neighborhood in the city—the North End. Mr. Johnson showed them the promised land of Albina, the old township absorbed into the city thirty years before in 1891. Williams Avenue and Russell Street became the center of the new Darktown.

The beautiful old Victorian houses filled up with African American families, and black-owned businesses sprang up along Williams, Vancouver, and Mississippi Avenues. Johnson's Keystone Investments became a center of brisk business in real estate under the impressive administration of Emanuel Green and Mary Johnson. At their peak around 1950, Keystone managed as many as seventy-seven separate music venues and bars, many with gambling, hundreds of commercial rentals, and a huge amount of housing. Mary specialized in furnished rentals and business opportunities. Emanuel focused on purchasing huge tracts of land near the eastside of the Burnside,

Steel, and Broadway bridges that could be turned into massive profit through city projects and urban renewal. Tom Johnson handled the political end, forging strong relationships with city and police powers such as Leon Jenkins, Al Winter, Mayor Fred Peterson, and others. Sam Shelby was heavily involved with security, and he was present a remarkable number of times when beatings or knifings occurred in the black community.

Tom Johnson may have dreamed of those future days as he surveyed the luxurious scene at his Greenfront Saloon in August 1932, but those days were far ahead and barely attainable. Mr. Johnson faced a hard limit as he learned "his place." Special Agent Kain and his men followed every move of driver Eugene Craver (alias Gene Carver), owner of Linger Longer Links amusement center on Northeast 27th Avenue, and his brother, Vern, who purchased and maintained cars for Gene's use through the garage on Northwest Broadway. Federal agents followed Craver to a house on North Vancouver, where Johnson's narcotics operation was based, and then watched him transfer cargo to the house next door, uncovering the still and brewery operation. The Feds prepared to pounce and had the Greenfront under surveillance the night the city's "official" gangster paid a visit.

Bobby Evans (real name Augustin Ardiss) came up the hard way on the streets. He shared a brotherhood, as strong as the bond among the Pullman porters, with the Jewish and Italian kids who grew up in the vital immigrant community of South Portland.[3] As a member of the Ex-Newsboys Association (E.N.A.), Evans was socially connected to some of the most influential and powerful men in the city. Membership of the E.N.A. included three mayors, George Baker, Fred Peterson, and Terry Schrunk; important businessmen such as J. J. Parker, the "Movie-house King," and Eddie Tonkin, the "Taxi King;" and criminals such as Bobby Evans, Abe Weinstein, Nick DePinto, and Jake Minsky.

Evans, a natural fighter, became a boxing champion before 1920, when he retired to become an official matchmaker for the Portland Boxing Commission, a powerful position in gambling-mad, boxing-crazy Portland. After Prohibition took effect and George Baker, another Ex-Newsboy, became mayor, Evans' fortunes rose. From his downtown gymnasium, the Shamrock Club, Evans became the city's "official gangster," balancing Police Chief Leon Jenkins' law enforcement efforts. Now near the end of Baker's third term as mayor, Evans and his men had become a bit power hungry and reckless. In an effort to thwart a popular recall petition that threatened the mayor and some of his most influential friends, Evans had his men break into the city attorney's office and brazenly steal the recall petitions. District Attorney Lotus Langley had just barely survived a recall election (they did not steal enough of his petitions) and was holding the lid on burglary charges. The mayor decided not to run for reelection. Evans was sure to lose his "official" status under the new mayor, and he made a grab for power at the expense of Tom Johnson. With the pressure already on the black community, it was time to try to make Johnson knuckle under.

Bobby Evans was escorted by an entourage of burly young men at 3 a.m. on Sunday, August 20, when his big car pulled up to the green building on Northwest Savier. Three days before Evans' visit, state and federal agents assisted by sheriff's deputies had raided the Greenfront. The raid was part of regular harassment as Helen Clark, daughter of Emanuel Green, and William Smith (real last name Johnson), Tom Johnson's younger brother, would face liquor charges from weekly raids on Mr. Johnson's drinking spots.

Police Chief Leon Jenkins looked forward to washing his hands of the dirty liquor business as the repeal of Prohibition approached and was powerless to help his old accomplice.

The people who accompanied the matchmaker on his visit to Mr. Johnson's club were an interesting group, mostly recruited from the youth-boxing program at Neighborhood House in South Portland. Young boxers Nick and Ray DePinto, Abe and Hyman Weinstein, and Jake Minsky all became important members of Evans' growing criminal empire. The Weinstein brothers had a state-wide fencing operation that recruited and trained its own burglars. They were not at the Greenfront, but Minsky and the DePinto brothers were there. Minsky was a cab-driver working for Eddie Tonkin's taxicab monopoly.[4] Nick and Ray DePinto had been on a bit of a rage, throwing their weight around all summer long, ever since the city attorney's office break-in they successfully pulled with assistance from Abe Weinstein's burglars. Nick shot Frank LaVodie, one of his accomplices on the "ballot job," when he caught him in bed with his wife, seriously wounding him. Ray and Nick then began a pressure campaign of brick-throwing and bombing against Tom Johnson's operation downtown—gambling, liquor, and prostitution at the Hotel Willard and a couple of nearby saloons.

Bobby Evans came to lay down the law that hot night in August as he entered the blues club, once again open after the raid. According to Sergeant Harry Parker, once Chief Jenkins' official driver, who told the story to *The Oregonian*, an intruder entered the room with a gun in his hand and took $250 out of Evans pocket. The "intruder" ignored the rest of the people in the room and spoke only with Evans. Sergeant Parker said that when Evans was interrogated about the meeting, he denied that he had been there. Tom Johnson was known for his coolness and sense of humor under pressure.[5] The intruder could have only been Mr. Johnson.

The visit ended with the DePinto brothers and Jake Minsky stealing all the money and booze in the place, except for the $250, which was still in Mr. Johnson's pocket. A few days later, Johnson closed the Greenfront for the duration, waiting out the federal agents. On December 15, 1933, U.S. Attorney Carl Donaugh ordered Portland Agent Kain to end his investigation, which was already languishing, concerning Tom Johnson *et al.*, writing, "No prosecution will be undertaken by this office in the above-named case insofar as the National Prohibition Act is concerned.... Therefore, case is closed."

By then, Minsky, both DePinto brothers, and Abe Weinstein were in jail for long stretches. Bobby Evans himself had managed to stay out of jail, but he was no longer a member of the Portland Boxing Commission, and it would be decades before he could rehabilitate himself into merely a "colorful" character; in that time, Mr. Johnson thrived.

Leon Jenkins was no longer chief, but he still ran the night shift and his disciples were scattered all through the police bureau. The new chief, Burton Lawson, was not from Portland and was easily fooled, not understanding the complex culture of the police bureau at all. The new mayor, Joseph Carson, embarrassed by the graft the city was taking in from vice operations, liked the autocratic powers the mayor had acquired over Baker's three terms. Johnson's relationship with the police bureau was strong, and he soon made an agreement with Al Winter, a Portland lawyer who controlled the Transcontinental Wire Service, providing information to the gambling parlors downtown. Winter and Johnson shared a love of gambling and horses, and by all accounts, they got along well. By 1935, Mr. Johnson had learned his place, but he had also expanded it a bit.

Tom Johnson was responsible for the exciting music scene in Portland, which drew stars like Billy Eckstein (right). (*Oregon Historical Society*)

The Golden West Hotel closed in 1931, but Johnson continued to use the big dining room there for meetings to discuss the development of "colored" Portland and to make plans for business and residential development around Williams Avenue and Russell Street. New Deal projects like the Bonneville Dam and Timberline Lodge on Mount Hood drew workers to the area and many of them settled in what Robert Dietsche calls "Jumptown." Tom Johnson supported the development of the black community by employing hundreds of musicians and service workers. He also provided low or no-interest loans to African American businesses and families in need. Bill McClendon, the publisher of the *Portland Observer*, described Mr. Johnson's operation as a "million dollar welfare system" and made it clear that Johnson supported community development even when it threatened his own interests, as long as it did not threaten them too much. For example, Johnson became one of the biggest financers of the National Urban League when it was established in Portland in 1946.

As Tom Johnson aged, the darker side of his business was more and more left to such underlings as Birches Bird, Herman "Candy" Canyon, and Roma "Big Poop" Ollison, especially after Emanuel Green died in 1954. The big man spent more and more time on his spread near Dallesport on the Columbia, where he raised his beloved horses. He moved there full-time in 1958, after his dirty dealings involving the construction of the Memorial Coliseum were exposed in the 1957 controversial Vice Scandal.[6]

Mr. Johnson ruthlessly enforced strict discipline, among his crew and in the neighborhood in general, but he could be lenient. Harry Vessel, a young tough who was wounded by Sam Shelby in the Porters Club in 1931, remained a thorn in the big man's side, causing trouble and stealing from Johnson's operation until his death in the early 1950s. Vessel, a World War II veteran, ended up buried at Willamette National Cemetery, instead of at the Portland Crematorium and Mausoleum, where Mr. Johnson could have got a group rate for all the people he knew who were interred there. Johnson, a World War I veteran, joined his old nemesis, Harry Vessel, in Willamette National Cemetery when he finally died in 1964 under what some thought were mysterious circumstances.

10

Follow Me Nowhere

Ask me no questions. Sing me no songs. Follow me nowhere. I'm already gone.

Nicole Baker

Heavy snow fell on the night of January 5, 1952, as police responded to a burglar alarm at Zidell Machinery and Supply on S.W. Moody Avenue. It was the third attempted entry at Zidell's and Portland detectives hoped they would finally get a break. Fresh footprints in the newly fallen snow led to a house on S.W. Hood Street. When no one answered the door, the police set up surveillance and watched the house for several days before they realized they had been fooled.

A few days later, on January 16, Detectives Ladd Hunt and Robert Shaylor got another break when eighteen-year-old William Dean Morris was picked up for trying to pass a check stolen in a burglary at the Laher Spring Tire Company. Held on a forgery charge, Morris was soon singing like a bird. He bragged about fooling the police by walking backward in his own footsteps on S.W. Hood Street, creating false tracks. He claimed he was the leader of a gang responsible for dozens of crimes and he led the police to a burned out safe in the woods nearby. Soon, five people were in custody, including Morris' partner, nineteen-year-old Robert Poitras. Hunt and Shaylor announced that they had solved more than sixty burglaries, dating back to December 1950.

On January 20, *The Oregonian* ran a long interview, accompanied by a large portrait, with William Morris, "ring-leader of teen-age outlaws." Morris portrayed himself as a go-getter who "can't just sit around a pool-hall all day doing nothing," and had to be "producing something every minute." He had been an A-student at Benson Polytechnic High School before dropping out at fifteen. Soon, he was managing two or three newspaper routes and driving a souped-up motorcycle to the library where he pored over books about safes and explosives. Arrested for burglary in 1948, "before he could try any of his newfound tricks," the fifteen-year-old was sent to the Oregon State Reformatory in Woodburn, OR. A novice at house-breaking, the young man received an advanced course in crime and was ready to go into business when he returned to Portland in 1950.

Right: Gary Gilmore attended Franklin High School in Portland for a short time. His main interest was crime. (*Multnomah County Library*)

Below: Broadway was the heart of Portland's entertainment district. It was also the hangout of a loose gang of teenagers who committed numerous crimes. (*Oregon Historical Society*)

Morris and Poitras pulled their first job together on December 28, 1950, when they broke into Flanagan's Garage on S.E. Belmont Street, stealing three car batteries. The two young thieves and their accomplices started an impressive series of burglaries (averaging five per month) lasting for more than a year. They robbed taverns, grocery stores, gas stations, and garages, stealing cash, checks, tools, car parts, groceries, liquor, and cigarettes. The professional quality of their work made the Portland police believe a gang of hardened yeggs was in town, but they could not pin any of the crimes on the usual suspects.

On December 9, 1951, the robbers hit Strohecker's Grocery on S.W. Patton Road and "kidnapped" a large safe containing more than $4,000 ($40,000 today). Unable to open the tough safe, they stashed it in the woods off of N.W. Cornell Road and concentrated their efforts on finding welding equipment that could help them get inside. That was what led them to Zidell's where they finally managed to get their hands on a portable acetylene torch. The torch burned some of the cash getting them in, but that was politely replaced when they took it to the local Federal Reserve Bank.

One thing Bill Morris wanted Portland to know was that he was his own boss. *The Oregonian* reported:

> He boiled angrily at mention of him as a graduate of the Broadway gang. 'Let's get one thing straight,' he exploded, 'So far as I know there's no such thing as an organized Broadway gang. It's just newspaper talk.'

Newspaper talk or not, people were listening.

Gary Gilmore, executed by the state of Utah in 1977, echoed *The Oregonian* story in his death-house interview with *Playboy* magazine. In 1952, Gilmore was an eleven-year-old paperboy, delivering *The Oregonian* in his S.E. Johnson Creek Boulevard neighborhood. After reading the interview with the young burglar and admiring his picture in "greaser" outfit and duck's ass haircut, young Gilmore began breaking into houses on his paper route, looking for handguns he could take down to Broadway in a bid to join the gang. As he told *Playboy* twenty-five years later, "I didn't even know if that gang existed.... I wanted to be part of an outfit like that ... the Broadway boys."

It was the first step on a road that led Gary Gilmore to a firing squad as the first man executed in the United States since the 1967 Supreme Court ruling against execution. Sentenced to death for two senseless crimes, Gilmore became a polarizing figure in the national debate over capital punishment. He also became an important symbol of rebellion for a generation that came of age in the late seventies and even a cultural icon. The donation of his eyes to a sightless man was immortalized in the punk rock song "Gary Gilmore's Eyes" by the Adverts. His life has been told in two brilliant books— *Executioner's Song* by Norman Mailer and *Shot in the Heart* by his younger brother, Mikal Gilmore. No matter where you stand in the debate on capital punishment, no one ever deserved execution more than Gary Gilmore. Even he knew that he posed extreme danger to society and could not continue to live in a free world. His story is as old as the city of Portland itself.

The legend of Portland's "Broadway Gang" goes back to the 1920s during the nation's first "juvenile delinquent" crisis after World War I. Young toughs with "effeminate" haircuts, distinctive clothes, and marijuana cigarettes began hanging out at the corner of S.W. Broadway and Yamhill, just blocks from the original Lincoln High School (now P.S.U.'s Lincoln Hall). Petty crime flourished and reports of car pilfering and pedestrian harassment rose in the popular theater district. The beginnings of a juvenile justice system were already in place in Portland, and in 1923, the police bureau assigned two officers to the new juvenile crime division.

The problem of "incorrigible" boys had been around at least since the 1870s when Police Chief James Lappeus would delivery fiery lectures to children caught chalking "dirty" words on downtown walls and fences. In 1891, the Oregon State Reformatory, for boys as young as eight, opened in Woodburn; it was colloquially known as Woodburn School. Portland's Boys and Girls Aid Society began sending unwanted children to the reform school for crimes ranging from "riding a streetcar without fare" to "trespassing to kill." Some boys were sent to Woodburn for sexual crimes like fornication, masturbation, and "homosexual perversion." Between 1891 and 1942, more than 4,000 boys went through the Woodburn School, most of them from Portland. The largest group, more than 1,100 of them, went to Woodburn not for specific crimes, but because their parents and authorities labeled them "incorrigible." Forty-three of them were said to be "beyond parental control."

In 1913, Lola Baldwin's Women's Protective Division of the Portland police took responsibility for these unwanted, uncontrollable children. At the same time, the Multnomah County courts began to handle "juvenile" cases separately from the adult courts and the State Industrial School for Girls in Hillcrest opened. Corporal punishment and hard labor were the main methods used to "reform" these children, but things were starting to change. In the 1930s, a "Give the Boys a Break" movement became popular and many people became convinced that society should try to understand the "juvenile delinquent." By World War II, juvenile corrections officials, like James Lamb, Multnomah County's chief juvenile probation officer, were looking to a "treatment" model of reform. When Lamb became the director of the Woodburn School in 1949, he began to try some of the experimental psychological techniques that were becoming available. In 1951, the school changed its name to the Maclaren School for Boys to reflect the new attitude.

Institutions change slowly and sometimes not at all. By the time fourteen-year-old Gary Gilmore arrived at Maclaren in 1955, he found a prison-like environment run by the toughest inmates. As he told *Playboy* in 1976, "The staff was local beer-drinking guys who put in their hours, and they didn't care if you did this and that."

In the twenty-first century, Maclaren School became the target of investigations into sexual and physical abuse by staff members as far back as the 1970s, but in 1954, hazing of new inmates included sexual abuse and rape. Gilmore denied it violently in his *Playboy* interview, saying he "would have killed someone" if they had tried to sexually assault him, but Norman Mailer documents a conversation in which Gilmore admitted that when he arrived at Maclaren, "a couple of boys held him down and he was raped. He hated it, he said, but would admit as he got older, he participated in the same game on the other side."

Mikal Gilmore, in his book *Shot in the Heart*, portrays his older brother as a man who had suffered a "history of destruction" and who was "afraid of everything but death." Mikal Gilmore, more than a decade younger than Gary, barely knew him, only spending time with him after his conviction for murder in Utah in 1976. Most of what he learned about his brother he learned during a process of discovering his own past and his own family. Early in the book, he ruminates on the course of Gary's life and where it went wrong:

> When and how does murder begin? Or to put it another way: Could I locate one moment where everything went wrong, one moment—or period of time—that might have made all the difference? And if I could find such a moment, would it be one inside Gary's own life? Or would it be one outside him—one, say, in the secret darkness of his own father's history?

Frank Gilmore, Gary's father, had been a successful circus clown, Laffo, with the Barnum and Bailey Circus until a bad fall and broken ankle ended his acrobatic career in 1910 and he soured on the entertainment business. Convinced by his mother, a spiritualist who worked under the name Baby Fay LaFoe, that he was the illegitimate son of Harry Houdini, Gilmore was an angry man with a strong grudge against his father, whoever he was. When Frank met Gary's mother, Bessie Brown, in Salt Lake City in 1937, he had been married "six or seven times" under as many different names. He was an "ad salesman," but he supported himself with a "hundred percent" scam; he would sell all the ads in an issue of a new magazine and then abscond with the collected funds. The couple led a peripatetic life, going from town to town under various names. Their second son, Gary, was born in Texas under the name Faye Robert Coffman in December 1940.

Weeks after the boy's birth, after the family had crossed the state line into New Mexico, Frank told Bessie she could rip up the baby's birth certificate. Bessie, who hated the name Frank had given their son, was relieved. She insisted that he should be named Gary after her favorite actor, Gary Cooper. Frank objected to the name, saying, "I'm not going to keep a son with that name." The name stayed, and after a short abandonment of his family, Frank returned. They continued their travels and finally settled in Portland in 1949 where Frank, nearly sixty years old, went into a legitimate business, publishing a *Building Codes Digest* in Portland and Seattle. Bessie and her growing brood of children settled into a big house on S.E. Johnson Creek Boulevard. Frank spent most of his time on the road.

Heavy drinking and violence against his wife and children were common when Frank was home. Gary and his brothers grew up afraid of their father; the neglect they received from him most of the time was welcome. Only when Gary started to have trouble with the law as a young teen did his father take an interest in him, defending him loudly against the police and spending money on lawyers. Gary, born under an alias, learned one important lesson from his father. As he told *Playboy* in 1976, "I always knew the law was silly as hell."

Gilmore told *Playboy* that going to Woodburn "was not a small thing in my life." With a measured I.Q. of 130 and artistic talent, Gary Gilmore was more intelligent than most of the boys that surrounded him. Years later the mother of the young woman, Nicole Baker, who tried to kill herself at his suggestion, compared Gilmore to Charles Manson in his ability to dominate people. At Woodburn, he began to develop his well-known charisma and dominant personality. His first year was rebellious; he attempted to escape four times before he realized he was just giving the authorities reason to keep him locked up. After four months of "good behavior," he was finally released in 1957. As he told *Playboy*, "That taught me that people like that were easily fooled."

He idolized the toughest, "hippest" boys imitating their style and attitude. In 1976, he told *Playboy*:

> Look, reform schools disseminate certain esoteric information. They sophisticate. A kid comes out of reform school and he's learned a few things he otherwise would have missed. And he identifies, usually, with the people who share that knowledge, the criminal element, or whatever you want to call it.

With duck's ass haircut, corduroy trousers, and spit-polished brogans, Gary Gilmore was what *The Oregonian* would have called a "graduate of the Broadway gang" a few years before. Elite Billiards on S.W. Broadway was still the tough hangout, soon to be eclipsed by the poolroom at Amato's Bowling Lanes on the eastside. Don Carpenter, in his 1964 novel *Hard Rain Falling*, depicts the scene on S.W. Broadway as a non-stop haze of alcohol, sex, and petty crime. He could have been writing about sixteen-year-old Gary Gilmore and his best buddy, another Maclaren graduate, Leroy Earp.

The two boys celebrated their freedom in February 1957 by stealing a car from Vest Motors on S.E. 82nd and taking it for a joy ride and car chase with the police that ended in a ditch. Alcohol probably contributed to the incident; Gilmore may have already started his habit of "pounding" beers (drinking one after another to maintain a slight alcoholic haze known as a "buzz").[1] Gary and Leroy Earp were remanded to the adult courts on an auto theft charge, but Multnomah County courts were lenient with young men who committed minor crimes under the influence of alcohol and Frank hired a good lawyer. They spent some time in Rocky Butte Jail but were soon released on a year's probation.

Alcohol was not the only substance that contributed to the crimes of Gary Gilmore. Drugs of all kinds, especially "grass" (cannabis) and "horse" (heroin), were easy to get in Portland in the 1950s. "Bennies", Benzedrine tablets, were popular with the Broadway boys and were most likely the pills Gary and Leroy had been taking. Benzedrine gives a speed-like rush that was very popular with World War II veterans who took it while in the service to stay awake. Before 1952, it was possible to buy over-the-counter nose drops containing 150 mg of Benzedrine. It became popular among the teenagers on Broadway to drink it in their Coca-Cola. With the usual dose of Benzedrine at 5 mg, a "benny coke" as they were called, had quite a kick.

In 1976, Gilmore accidentally shot himself in the hand while trying to hide the weapon he used to kill his second murder victim, Bennie Bushnell. That was not the first time he injured someone with careless handling of a weapon. In July 1957, he accidentally shot Leroy Earp in the side while they were walking together on S.E. 50th Avenue, not far from Gilmore's home. When the cops showed up, Gilmore tried to laugh it off, saying he had been "playing" with the gun. The police were suspicious, though, because the two teenage boys were out at 2.30 in the morning and the 0.38 caliber handgun in their possession had been stolen from a nearby used-car lot. Gilmore ended up back in Rocky Butte jail, this time on a burglary charge.

While Gilmore was at Rocky Butte another man, Cleophis Womack, was being held there on a charge of armed robbery. It is not certain that he and Gary met, but it is the

Gilmore, Frank   **Gilmore, Gary**   **Gilmore, Jerry**

The three Gilmore brothers started school together as freshmen at Franklin High School in 1955. They soon became a discipline problem. (*Multnomah County Library*)

first time we can be sure their paths crossed. Womack returned from the Korean War in 1953, recovering from a head injury. Over the next few years, he began to have temper problems that resulted in violent incidents, until he was finally arrested in June 1957 for beating and threatening Frank J. Guncheck with a switchblade knife, while stealing his watch and $180 in cash. It would be a few years before Gilmore and Womack teamed up and their paths would cross more than once.

Multnomah County courts could be lenient with troubled young men, but Gary Gilmore was reaching the limits. This time, his dad's good lawyer could only get him off with a year in county jail and Gary stayed in Rocky Butte. At the age of sixteen, it was his first serious jail time. It did not help. Mikal Gilmore, who was not yet ten years old, describes the situation in his house after his brother got out of jail. Violent fights, high tension, and outrageous behavior on Gary's part were typical. The seventeen-year-old was definitely pounding beers by this time, and he had probably already started his habit of walking into a store with a threatening expression and stoically walking out with six-packs of beer. Mikal remembers a deep conversation with his drunken older brother who imparted one of the few lessons he remembered ever hearing from him:

> 'You have to learn to be hard,' he said, '... No pain, no anger, nothing.... if anyone wants to beat you up, even if they hold you down and want to kick you, you have to let them.... It's the only way you'll survive.'

In September 1959, Gary was back in court on two counts of larceny. In October, the Multnomah County grand jury recommended a work camp for first offenders and persons convicted of minor crimes. A work camp would provide a better living environment and "remove young offenders from the undesirable influence which living closely with hardened criminals must surely have." The same grand jury indicted eighteen-year-old Gary Gilmore for contributing to the delinquency of a minor. According to Mikal Gilmore, this incident, with a fifteen-year-old girl, produced Gilmore's only child, a son that was born out of state and never had contact with his father's family. Gilmore reminisced about these days in his *Playboy* interview: "I smoked, drank, shot heroin, smoked weed, took speed, got into fights, chased and caught pretty little broads. I stole, robbed and gambled and went to Fats Domino and Gene Vincent concerts."

The good times came to an end in September 1960 when Gilmore was sentenced to the Oregon State Correctional Institution (O.S.C.I.) on a charge of larceny. Most likely, his crime was stealing a car. Gilmore took great pride in his car theft abilities, although he probably never had a driver's license and never became a good driver. Opened the year before, O.S.C.I. was a medium-security facility in Salem, designed to hold youthful offenders, especially those who had been in youth facilities like Maclaren School. It was another step in Gilmore's progress through the corrections system.

After serving eighteen months at O.S.C.I., Gilmore was released in February 1962. Picked up right away on a charge of driving without a license, he was back in Rocky Butte jail when his father died of cancer. Frank Gilmore's death was a traumatic event for his son. Gary tried to kill himself when he found out, breaking a lightbulb in his cell and slashing his wrists deeply, before waking his cellmate who then summoned help. It was the first in a long series of suicidal gestures, which always fell short of fatality. He tried to kill himself twice while in prison in Utah awaiting execution. Even his execution, in some ways, could be considered suicide. Bullets fired into the heads of Max Jensen and Bennie Bushnell, the two robbery victims Gilmore killed in Utah, might as well have been shot into his own skull.

Settling into a house on S.E. Oatfield Road, twenty-one-year-old Gary Gilmore and his new partner, Cleophis Womack, more than a decade older, ranged over Portland and the surrounding towns in a small crime wave. Stealing cars and robbing grocery stores for liquor and cigarettes were their main work, but "hanging out" was their main occupation. By 1962, the scene on S.W. Broadway had changed. Teenage wannabe gangsters still hung out there, but there was hardly any activity on the sidewalks. The car was king as teenagers cruised "the gut" along S.W. Broadway and hung out at drive-in restaurants or the new Lloyd Center mall. Elite Billiards moved to a new location on S.W. Park Avenue and the tough boys drifted to the east side of the Willamette River, where Amato's Lanes and Restaurant on S.E. 12th provided bowling, pool, drinks, and an intense parking lot drug-dealing scene. Hash (concentrated cannabis) and acid (LSD-25) were the popular new drugs, but grass, horse, and speed were always available.

It is interesting to note Gary Gilmore's arrests for crimes almost always occurred in the month of September, especially before he was sentenced to the Oregon State Prison in 1964. In September 1963, Gary and Cleophis spotted an older man with a prosperous look, Carl Thelin, in the parking lot of the Oak Grove Shopping Center near Milwaukie, south of Portland. Following Thelin, they watched him cash a payroll check and then trailed him as he drove to his home between Milwaukie and Oregon City. Armed with

As cars came to dominate culture, Broadway became a less popular hangout for young criminals on foot as they migrated to the east side of the river. (*Oregon Historical Society*)

metal pipes, the two robbers confronted Thelin and his wife in their garage. Thelin resisted and was beaten senseless and robbed.

In 1976, Gilmore told *Playboy*, "I got away with a couple things. I ain't a great thief. I'm impulsive. Don't plan, don't think. You don't have to be super-intelligent to get away with shit, you just have to think."

Gary and Cleophis thought nothing of what they did. A security guard spotted them in the parking lot trailing the older man. Within thirty minutes of the crime, Clackamas County deputies were at Gilmore's house where they found a car stolen in North Portland; the trunk and back seat were stuffed with cigarette and liquor cartons stolen during a burglary at Ward Market on S.E. 37th.

Clackamas County was not as lenient on young criminals, especially if they were from Portland, but Gary had a new trick up his sleeve. Charged with armed robbery and assault he pled insanity, citing several suicide attempts. Womack was considered a first offender (overlooking at least two previous arrests) and the judge sentenced him to three years at O.S.C.I. Thirty-three-year-old Womack begged the judge not to send him "down there with them boys." The judge relented and Womack went to the Oregon State Penitentiary. Gilmore was sent to the Dammasch State Hospital for psychological evaluation.

Dammasch State Hospital, a mental hospital, asylum, and education center in Wilsonville, operated between 1961 and 1995. Like the Oregon State Hospital in Salem, Dammasch used drug therapy, electro-shock, surgery, isolation, and "occupational" therapy with the goal of keeping their inmates under control. From Ken Kesey's 1962 novel, *One Flew Over the Cuckoo's Nest*, to the 1993 *Five Deaths at Dammasch Hospital: A Question of Responsibility*, horrifying abuses have been told and documented in the Oregon State hospital system. It was probably at Dammasch that Gilmore was first drugged to keep him under control. The popular drug in 1964 was thorazine. A few years later after the 1971 riot at the Oregon State Prison, Gilmore received "treatment" with prolixin, a much more powerful and long-lasting tranquilizer.[2] Family members claimed that Gary's personality changed significantly after the prolixin, as if he didn't care about anything at all anymore. Like Kesey's character McMurphy, Gary Gilmore probably thought the hospital would be easier to escape from than the Oregon State Prison, where he knew he was headed. He did escape in March 1964.

The twenty-three-year-old Gary Gilmore had already spent 20 percent of his life institutionalized, yet that percentage was about to go way up. He only stayed out one day, probably visiting Bessie, who left penniless after Frank's death lost their home and lived in a trailer park near Milwaukie with thirteen-year-old Mikal. The next day, Gary turned himself in and suffered the consequences. He got fifteen years in the State Penitentiary. It was a life sentence. Twelve years later, he was dead.

The life of Gary Gilmore from the Oregon State Prison to the United States Penitentiary in Marion, Illinois, to his execution at the Utah State Prison in Draper on January 17, 1977, has been told well. He spent only two brief periods outside of prison in those years, including one in 1970 when he qualified for a student release program under the condition he register at University of Oregon in Eugene. He spent about ninety days in Portland without registering for school and was picked up for a burglary. In 1976, he was released from the federal prison in Marion on parole to Provo, Utah. While he was on parole, he committed the crimes for which he was executed—the murders of Max Jensen and Bennie Bushnell.

The people whom Gary Gilmore called friends could fill an entire new book. Leroy Earp, Gilmore's teenage friend from Maclaren, went to the Oregon State Penitentiary in 1966 on a life sentence for the rape and murder of Carol Jean Charlson, a twenty-six-year-old S.E. Portland waitress. Escaping several times, Earp served fourteen years before release on parole in 1980. Earp admitted to a psychiatrist during his incarceration that he was "quite fearful of the lack of control that would be imposed on me on the outside." Returning to Portland, Earp was hired as a custodian at Rex Putnam High School, after claiming he had worked as a janitor for the state for the last fourteen years. In 1982, he murdered Rex Putnam physical education teacher Ann Johnette Perry and once again returned to the controlled environment of prison he seemed to value. Vincent "Iceman" Capitan, who went to the Oregon State Prison in 1969 for the murder of Carlos Mendoza and then became a Portland drug-kingpin working with the Outsiders Motorcycle Club after his release was a friend of Gary Gilmore. Another friend was revolutionary bank robber Stephen Kessler, who tried to renounce his citizenship in 1963 so he could "fight for communism with the East Germans." Kessler, who became notorious for his prison-breaks, had a brief period of fame when attorney William Kunstler represented him in his struggles with the Oregon State Prison.

After his fourteenth birthday, Gary Gilmore never spent a full year outside the walls of an institution. He died at the age of thirty-five. The "rebel myth"—in which a steadfast person refuses to compromise belief at all costs—dominated Gilmore's life and his picture of himself. Norman Mailer's book clearly shows how Gilmore attempted to control the public's perception of him and what he was doing to reinforce this myth. Gilmore's case dominated the news in 1976, the same year in which the 1975 film version of *One Flew Over the Cuckoo's Nest* dominated the Academy Awards in Hollywood. Jack Nicholson's portrayal of McMurphy, who could have been based on the young Gary Gilmore, showed that he had to die in order to liberate the protagonist, Chief Broom. In the same way, Gilmore's execution dramatized the "sacrifice" of the criminal in order to liberate society, but Max Jensen and Bennie Bushnell sacrificed as much or more by their senseless deaths.

11

THE IN CROWD

Our share is always the biggest amount.

Billy Paige, The In Crowd

The house on North Vancouver Avenue had tight security. Metal bars covered the windows, and the plain wooden door had several dead-bolt locks securing it. Traffic was regular with cars stopping in front day and night while people made quick visits. It was a new phenomenon in Portland, a drug house, where heroin and the newly popular methamphetamine (crank) could be purchased any time. The owner of the house, forty-seven-year-old Harold "Slick Willie" Penland, had good reason to be paranoid. Once a famous boxer and lightweight champion of Oregon and Washington known as Willie "Battling" Nelson, Penland had spent the last twenty years developing a reputation as one of Portland's most violent sex offenders, most prolific drug dealers, and most knowledgeable police informers. Phil Stanford, the chronicler of Portland's underworld, called Penland, "one of the truly transcendent thugs in Portland history. And what makes it so much more remarkable is that much of the time he was working hand-in-glove with the police."

A lot of people had good reason to want Penland dead. Laura, his twenty-seven-year-old wife, knew that. She would have only opened the door to someone she knew and trusted.

That was what she did on the night of Saturday, June 4, 1983. We know she answered the door because Willie was upstairs working out in "gravity boots," hanging upside down. Laura Liska Penland was from one of Portland's "good" families. She graduated from Marylhurst College and was a member of the Multnomah Athletic Club, but like so many daughters of upper-middle-class families, she became addicted to drugs and bad men. The killers she let into the house tried to save her from what they were going to do. Laura was supposed to go out to dinner with a friend that night, but she was not feeling well and stayed home. It was too late for her. Phil Stanford says one of the killers let her shoot up drugs before they did their job. "Take as much as you want," he said, "Because it doesn't really matter anymore." It did not matter; there would be no witnesses left alive.

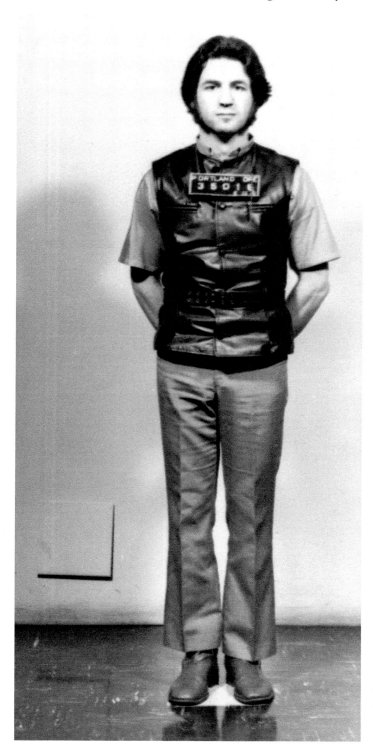

Harold "Slick Willie" Penland (a.k.a. Willie Nelson)—one of the truly transcendent thugs of Portland history. (*Photo courtesy of Phil Stanford*)

Getting the drop on Willie while he was in gravity boots was a lucky break for the killers. Willie was known for being sneaky, a guy who loved a sucker punch. Buddy Moore, one of Willie's friends from St. Johns told Phil Stanford:

> When Willie's getting ready to throw a sucker punch, he folds his arms on his chest, as if he were calmly contemplating the situation. But he's really just waiting till the guy is in range, then bang, straight out comes the right, and by all accounts he can hit like a mule.

Musician Todd Snider, who knew Willie as a friend of his father's when he was a child, immortalized Slick Willie's sneakiness in the song "Unorganized Crime," but "the trick only worked about half the time."[1] As Snider says in the song, "Everyone around Portland knew he was a low-life to say the least" and "there'd be too many suspects to solve the crime."

Suspects there were. Vincent Capitan, who went to prison in 1969 for killing Carlos Mendoza after which he dubbed himself "the Iceman," ran the biggest methamphetamine operation in the city and he held personal and professional grudges against Willie that could have led to murder. The murderous narcotics cops, Neil "Gearshift" Gearhart and Scott "Big Red" Deppe, were uneasy friends of Willie's, but that would not rule out murder with them. His own heroin distributor, Ben Willis, might have wanted him dead, and John King, who worked at an 82nd Avenue used car lot, was rumored to know how to do it. Even the kid of one of his friends, Todd Snider, said in the song about Willie, "I'm the one who killed Slick Willie … and I don't feel guilty. If I could I would do it again." It seemed like everyone wanted old Willie dead and the Portland cops did not really care about pinning it on anyone. No one cared. *The Oregonian* even got his name wrong in their first report of the death, calling him Howard Penland. No one remembered the young boxer on the way up, and anyone who remembered who Willie had become was glad he was dead. The double homicide was filed away as Cold Case Nos 834492 and 834493 and that is where it has stayed for forty years.

Yet thirty years before, *The Oregonian* could not get enough of the talented welterweight who transferred from a Salem High School to Lincoln High for his senior year in 1954. The bland picture of his smiling "jock" face in the Lincoln yearbook shows his physical presence which intimidated, but it does not even hint at the sadistic streak that made Willie like to hurt people. As a boxer, he was good. He fought thirty bouts and won twenty-four, knocking out eight opponents. In February 1957, he was at the top of his game. At twenty-one, he held the welterweight championship in Oregon and Washington and although he had a few draws, he had never been beaten. We do not know where he got his name, but KVAN radio, the country/western station from Vancouver, featured a disc jockey called Wee Willie Nelson, who would soon cut his first record on his way to becoming a national icon.[2] We do not know if Slick Willie liked country music, but he fought all his fights under the name Willie "Battling" Nelson and was known as Willie for the rest of his life.

Slick Willie committed a lot of different types of crime, but the one he started with is the one he always came back to—rape. It is difficult to write about the history of rape because the crime is rarely reported and not usually mentioned in the newspapers; euphemisms were often used even in police reports. We do not know the details of the case or the name of Willie's first victim, but we know he was charged with rape in February 1957, and a couple of weeks later, the charge was dropped when the Multnomah County Grand Jury failed to indict him. He went to Eastern Oregon State Hospital for psychological evaluation during this case. They diagnosed "chronic brain syndrome associated with brain trauma." Willie always claimed it was the rape accusation that ended his fighting career, but the real problem is that he started losing his fights. In October 1957, Willie lost his first bout, which was to Nat Simon. He would only fight professionally twice more, and he lost both bouts. His attention was elsewhere.

Willie started his boxing at the Police Athletic League (P.A.L.) gym in southeast Portland. P.A.L. was born in New York City in 1943 as one of Mayor Fiorello LaGuardia's war measures. It was designed to divert "underprivileged" young men from delinquency by teaching them to box. Before the war was over, the idea had spread to cities all over the country. In Portland, a popular lightweight boxer named Mason "Mickey" Pease, who joined the police bureau in 1943, organized the P.A.L. in his gym, located in the Dekum Building, in 1945. Pease devoted the next fifteen years to P.A.L. and the police juvenile division. The boys who participated in P.A.L. not only had great opportunities to get to know Portland police officers they were made "junior deputies" of the sheriff's department.

Criminal exploitation of youth athletic programs goes back a long way in Portland. Bobby Evans, Portland's crime boss during Mayor George Baker's administration, may have been the first to recruit young men from the boxing and basketball teams at Neighborhood House, South Portland's settlement house based on the work of Chicago's Jane Addams. The Weinstein and DePinto brothers were all recruited from Neighborhood House and became key members of Evans' crime gang.[3]

Evans had been one of the founding members of Portland's Ex-Newsboys Association, an organization whose members permeated both the city's business and crime communities. His heirs, for the most part, were also Ex-Newsboys and some of them were involved with P.A.L. Paul Ailes, who became Oregon's "concessions king" and created Portland Meadows, The Multnomah County Kennel Club, and Portland International Raceway, was an active and enthusiastic supporter of P.A.L., and he is known to have recruited members of his North Portland crime ring from the boxing team.

Downtown restauranteur John Runstein (a.k.a. Johnny Boston) was also a member of P.A.L. and suspected of criminal connections. Boston ran card rooms in several locations downtown, which were technically illegal, but openly tolerated by the police bureau. In 1965, he bought Dunkin's Retreat, which was the most notorious hangout for organized crime figures in the city, from mobster Al Winter. It is not hard to see that many of the members of the P.A.L. boxing team later had criminal careers and received special protection from prosecution.

The best illustration of the protection criminals like Slick Willie enjoyed is an event in September 1961. It happened on North Failing Street, across the street from Unthank Park. Officers from the vice squad raided an after-hours club in the neighborhood and then heard a commotion—loud noises and profanity—coming from a house nearby. North Portland was full of drinking establishments that stayed open after closing hours

Boxing at the Police Athletic League was a popular pastime for "disadvantaged" young men in the 1940s and '50s. It was also a great place for criminals to recruit young men as enforcers. (*Oregon Historical Society*)

and vice cops often raided the unprotected ones when they needed to up their arrest numbers. The house where the noise originated seems to have had special status; either it was an after-hours club or a safe house (either way a lot of criminals lived there over the years). The vice cops probably did not realize what they were getting into when they confronted the drunken "near riot."

The Oregonian reported the affair with an odd mixture of sensationalism and discretion. "One of the officers was dragged up a flight of stairs to a porch, beaten, then grabbed by the arms and legs and thrown back to the sidewalk," the paper reported without naming the officers involved. Two other officers, who attempted to rescue their partner, were treated the same way. Ten or twelve people ran from the scene, but Willie Nelson and five of his friends were arrested after the scuffle and a failed attempt to rescue the people detained in the earlier after-hours raid. You might think six drunken men who systematically assaulted the police would face serious charges, but you would be wrong in this case.

Harold Penland transferred from Salem to Lincoln High School in Portland for his senior year. He was already boxing and, under the name "Battlin' Willie Nelson," he would soon become a recognized semi-professional fighter. (*Multnomah County Library*)

Charges were dropped against George Player, who lived in the house on N. Failing, the five others were convicted of disorderly conduct. Two of them were fined less than $50. Two were fined $50 and sentenced to sixty days in jail, with forty days suspended; their jail sentences were equal to the time they had already served. Willie Nelson got the worst of it—$100 fine and ninety days, forty-five suspended. Willie was working for Elmo Jacks, a local nightclub owner who ran a counterfeiting ring and his protection was good.

Willie was having serious legal trouble in 1961, though. In October 1960, he beat John Wasson so badly in a S.E. 82nd Avenue bar that Wasson was hospitalized. When the police arrived Willie ran, losing his pursuers as he jumped over a fence into the backyard of Sheriff's Deputy Howard Bergstrom. Willie hid in the recreation room of Bergstrom's house, but when Bergstrom's wife, Margaret, and their ten-year-old daughter found him there, Willie grabbed the girl and threatened her life before bolting from the house into the arms of two other deputies who were searching for him. Willie went back to Eastern State Hospital for a short time, but no charges were pursued. In March 1961, still on probation, Willie forced his way into the apartment of a twenty-three-year-old waitress and raped her. He went back to the state hospital for more evaluation, but eventually in December 1962, he was convicted of rape and given three years' probation. You can understand why he thought the law was a joke.

Portland Police officer Don DuPay remembers a near fatal encounter with Slick Willie that occurred in February 1964 when DuPay had been on the force almost three years. Working the traffic detail, DuPay was parked in an unmarked car on S.E. 72nd Avenue near Woodstock when a 1959 Cadillac sped through the stop sign right in front of him. Following the Cadillac, DuPay clocked it doing 65 miles per hour as it blew past the stop sign at S.E. Duke. The car finally stopped near S.E. Flavel, and DuPay found a stinking drunk, but sharply dressed Willie Nelson at the wheel. "I can't go to jail," Willie said. "The hell you won't," DuPay answered, pushing him against the side of the car.

A knife flashed as Willie tried to stab DuPay in the belly. A hard scuffle ensued. Willie's probation officer, Loren F. Bridge, reported, "The officer wrestled with the driver in hopes of subduing him, and DuPay states that he hit the subject's head against the hood of the police car seven or eight times in order to subdue him." Finally, the ex-professional boxer caught DuPay's wrist in a lock-hold and broke away, fleeing into a clump of trees. DuPay fired a shot at the fleeing suspect, managing to put a bullet through Willie's sports coat, but without hitting him. DuPay needed medical treatment for his wrist afterward. As Don DuPay likes to say, "Police work is basically a contact sport."

You might think that assault with a deadly weapon against a police officer might result in serious charges for a guy on probation for a rape conviction, but not for Slick Willie. Arrested by detectives the next day, he claimed it never happened. He said he spent the night with Beatrice Jacks, wife of his boss Elmo Jacks. It was her Cadillac that DuPay impounded after the traffic stop, so detectives arrested Willie. He was charged with "escape and evasion of an officer" and released on $2,500 bail. Probation officer Bridge reported that "he is due to be arraigned before a Grand Jury in the near future." That was the last of it.

Elmo Jacks owned a notorious club on N.E. Sandy Boulevard, Elmo's Western Club, a well-known gangster hangout. Willie worked as a parking attendant and bouncer at the Western Club. Elmo's was "wide-open" providing gambling, women and drugs along with its booze, but most people did not know that Jacks' real business was counterfeiting $10 and $20 bills. In 1959, Jacks was arrested with printing plates for both kinds of bills, but his lawyer was good, so he only got probation. In 1964, Jacks was busted again with phony $10 bills in his possession. This time, he went to federal prison for two years. It was bad news for Slick Willie.

One year after the encounter with Officer DuPay, in February, 1965, Special Police Officer Vern W. Rake was driving on N.E. Union Avenue (now MLK Jr. Blvd) when Slick Willie nearly hit his car while driving the wrong way on the one-way street. Willie's car sped off and Rake turned onto N.E. Grand, one block east. Willie, driving the wrong way on another one-way street, almost hit him again and Rake forced him to the curb. Willie jumped out of his car and punched Rake, knocking him to the ground. Rake, a glorified security guard, chased Willie toward N.E. Hancock Street, where two regular officers finally subdued and handcuffed him. With his protector in federal prison, it was the last straw for Slick Willie. His probation was revoked, and he went to the Oregon State Penitentiary to serve his three-year sentence for rape.

Released from Oregon State Prison in April 1967, Willie found a new protector, Billy Moe, a Chinese-American restauranteur. For decades, Moe's family had been associated with the powerful Hop Sing Tong. His older brother, Fred (a.k.a. Moe Yim), was a key figure in the smuggling operation that brought heroin to Portland from China. Fred Moe died in a spectacular suicide in 1959, after being arrested in a drug raid that the C.I.A. claimed proved Red China (The People's Republic of China) was responsible for bringing heroin into the country.[4] From 1965–1971, Moe's restaurant, Bill's Gold Coin, on West Burnside was a popular hangout for Portland's high-rollers and also the center of prostitution and drugs in Portland. Don DuPay remembers the flashy cars parked in the lot at the Gold Coin. It was a regular stop on the "gangster loop," which included the Three Star on Barbur Boulevard, the White Elephant in Beaverton, and Van's Olympic Room on North Vancouver Avenue.

Bill Moe's influence was great. Not only was he associated with the powerful Hop Sing Tong, but his relationship with George Yerkovich, city auditor, provided extra influence with the city. Part of Yerkovich's job was hooking up visiting dignitaries with the girls who were always available in the lounge at Bill's Gold Coin. In addition, Phil Stanford relates in *Rose City Vice* that Moe used blackmail against government officials and businessmen to enhance his influence. For several years, Billy Moe was untouchable.

Slick Willie worked in the parking lot at the Gold Coin, parking cars, but that was not all he did. Willie would copy house keys from the key rings of patrons who parked their cars in his lot and later, with the help of his friends Jerry Rogers and Phillip "Frenchie" LeBrun, burglarize their homes. Willie did not neglect his favorite crime, either. He regularly raped the women who worked at the Gold Coin, warning them not to say anything. Otherwise, their husbands or boyfriends might "do something stupid" and have to be killed.

On December 9, 1969, Willie walked into an "undercover store" on N.E. Glisan and offered several household items for sale. Long before these operations were known as "stings" after the 1973 film, the Portland police ran second-hand stores staffed by undercover officers to recover goods from home burglaries.[5] Slick Willie was very open with the "clerk" at the store saying that he used a "pass key" to enter a house on S.E. 90th Drive and even described the inside of the house. When he was arrested for selling stolen goods, Willie claimed it was a "bum rap," but the police also found in his possession a Kodak slide projector and other electronic equipment taken in another November burglary. His burglary partner, LeBrun, received a four-year sentence, but Willie's probation record shows no jail time after this arrest. It was probably around this time that he started working as an informer for P.P.B. narcotics detective John Giani.

The P.P.B. detective division began with three members—Joe Day, Frank Snow, and Jack Kerrigan—in 1894. All three detectives relied on the "stool pigeon system," where they cultivated relationships with criminals of various kinds and protected them from prosecution as long as they fed the detectives information on rival criminals. By 1905, the "inspectors bureau" had tripled in size, and it seemed like most of the crime in the city was being conducted by men who could not be prosecuted because of their close relationships with detectives. In August 1905, lower-ranking officers arrested "stool pigeons" Bob Lucas and Frank Lamb and forced prosecution for various crimes. It was one of the biggest scandals of Mayor Harry Lane's administration as he forced Detective Joe Day to back down on protecting Lucas and tried to bring the detectives under control.

It appeared to be a victory for Mayor Lane, but the detective bureau never stopped the stool-pigeon system; they just became a little more discreet about it. In the 1920s, Mayor Baker made the system official with "the mayor's secret police," a force of undercover operatives, like John "Handsome Hans" Fagerlie and Anna Schrader, who helped the mayor gain and keep control of the illegal liquor trade during prohibition.

The police bureau detective division was organized in 1894 and soon grew into an important part of the bureau. (*Portland Police Historical Society*)

Detective Joe Day (front row fourth from right) was an important member of the detective squad, gaining international attention for his work. (*Portland Police Historical Society*)

Fagerlie, Schrader, and several other "private detectives" were paid from special city appropriations, received police training and many of them conducted their own illegal enterprises.[6] George Baker's ideas of "law enforcement" were discredited in the 1930s and the stool-pigeon system had to go back underground, but it held on, and by the 1970s, it was as popular with police detectives as it had ever been.

Phil Stanford describes John "Uncle Johnny" Giani as "a little crooked." Like many of the detectives who came up through the Vice Squad, Giani had a small interest in prostitution, collecting hundreds of dollars a week for protecting his favorite girls. Like many of the city's narcotics detectives, Giani was known to take a little something for himself, either drugs or merchandise, when he made an arrest. Angela Mastne, who was involved in the drug business with her husband Larry, told Phil Stanford about the time Giani arrested them, but let them off after taking all the camping equipment from their van. This traditional "light graft" goes back to the days of Police Chief James Lappeus in the 1860s, but some of the younger detectives were ready to go to new heights.

Neil Gearhart, of the Special Investigations Division (S.I.D.), and Scott Deppe, a North Precinct officer working in narcotics, saw their work to suppress drug dealers as a crusade. Their enthusiasm and brutality earned them the nicknames "Gearshift" and "Big Red" as they became a familiar presence in Portland's underworld. Like most "holy warriors," Gearhart and Deppe found themselves becoming the thing they fought as they began to take over the drug business they worked so hard to suppress. There are multiple accounts of Portlanders arrested with small amounts of marijuana being forced to sell heroin and pills and turn over the money to Gearshift and Big Red. The two police officers have even been suspected of at least five (and probably quite a few more) murders. It all came to a head in December 1979 with the botched raid at the Outsiders Motorcycle Club and the death of Officer David Crowther, but that is getting ahead of the story.

On probation after the 1969 burglary case, Slick Willie had to report his activities to probation officer Richard E. Whipple, so we have a cleaned-up report of what Willie was up to in the 1970s. In 1971, he and Jerry Rogers, his old burglary buddy from the Gold Coin parking lot, went into business together with the Sultan's Harem, a chain of massage parlors financed by attorney George Desbrisay. Desbrisay, a former longshoreman, had great connections with the city and put together financing for many of the narcotics shipments coming into Portland. He used the Sultan's Harem to launder some of the money from his drug operations. Jerry Rogers told Phil Stanford that the Sultan's Harem brought in about $750,000 per year and that Desbrisay got almost all of it.

Slick Willie was doing okay, though. With protection from Giani and Desbrisay, he did not have much to worry about as he developed his heroin distribution business in North Portland. Turning over his rivals, including Jerry Rogers, to Giani reduced the competition and soon he had most of the market. Willie reported to Probation Officer Whipple that after the massage parlors closed down in 1973, he went into the "fish business." He even got several travel authorizations to go out of state to acquire "fish contracts." Willie's probation ended in 1976, and that was about the end of his legal troubles.

By 1979, Willie was moving a lot of heroin through his house on North Lombard Street and was ready for a new product. Crank (methamphetamine) was a popular fad among professional athletes, who saw it as a performance-enhancing drug, and was on the verge of becoming the most popular illegal drug among the working class. When Vincent "Iceman" Capitan got out of the state penitentiary, after serving less than ten years of a life sentence for murder, he was ready to put his new meth-cooking skills to use and soon set up production in a mobile home in Molalla, a rural community south of Portland. Using the Outsiders Motorcycle Club of St. Johns for transportation and security, Capitan began to supply Portland with the popular new drug. Slick Willie became one of the biggest wholesalers of Capitan's product.

Everything went smoothly until Capitan caught Slick Willie in bed with his girlfriend, Leslie Jefferson, who ran a call-girl operation from the Habitat Apartments. Capitan threatened to kill Willie, and Willie knew he was crazy enough to try it. He called his old buddy John Giani to turn in Capitan, who was still on probation. Giani had recently been promoted from narcotics and he got Willie in touch with a couple of guys from the Special Investigations Division, Gearhart and Deppe. Phil Stanford tells the story in *Rose City Vice* how Gearhart and Deppe used Slick Willie to frame Capitan and the Outsiders for heroin distribution and take over their methamphetamine operation. He also tells how the whole thing came apart during the trial of Outsiders member Robert "Pigpen" Christopher for shooting officer Dan Crowther. You should read it.

By the time Slick Willie married Laura Liska in 1981, he was sitting pretty. With the backing of Gearhart and Deppe Willie enjoyed a status similar to the city's "official bootlegger" of Prohibition, Bobby Evans, another ex-boxer. Although the illegal drug trade was not directed from City Hall, the way the illegal booze trade had often been, Slick Willie's drug operation was nearly as untouchable. If he had not been addicted to burglary and one-upsmanship, Willie might still be alive today.

Phil Stanford talked to a lot of people who knew Willie Nelson during his life and many of them believed it was his heroin distributor, Ben Willis, who had him killed. According to the story, Willis went on vacation and Willie, being Willie, broke into his house and stole his stuff. Willie did not notice the security camera Willis had set up and

Harold Penland as he appeared in 1970. (*Photo courtesy of Phil Stanford*)

when Ben returned from vacation, he knew right away it was Slick Willie who hit his house. That was why he called John King and put a contract on Willie's life.

John Burns King, born in Eugene in 1937, served in the army in the 1960s and was in prison in New York State in the early seventies. It is very difficult to find any information on King's military or criminal career and he claimed that the C.I.A. helped him get out of prison because he did occasional "jobs" for them. According to his 2000 obituary in *The Oregonian*, Burns moved to Portland in 1975 and worked as a self-employed used car dealer until his retirement in 1999. According to rumors, John King was a killer for hire.

It might have been John King who arrived at the drug house on North Vancouver that Saturday night in 1983. Laura would have let him in because he often ran errands for Ben Willis. It might have been John King who went upstairs and pumped six bullets into Slick Willie, hanging upside down in his gravity boots. It might have been John's younger brother Phil, who stayed in the kitchen with Laura while she shot up before they killed her. Everybody involved is dead now, so we will never know for sure.

12

THE ANIMAL

That was part of my problem before. I didn't know what I wanted to do.

Douglas Franklin Wright

Tony Shawn Nelson, like many U.S. Army veterans in the 1980s, had a difficult time coming back home and adapting to civilian life. A member of the Makah Tribe born in Port Angeles, WA, in 1960, Nelson moved with his adoptive family to Portland when he was five years old. Twenty-five years later, in 1991, he was back in Portland, but estranged from his family. Since his discharge from the army, Nelson lived a transient life, supporting himself as a seasonal firefighter and with whatever jobs he could find that allowed him to work outdoors. It was a precarious and lonely existence, and in October 1991, he was staying at the Salvation Army Recovery Inn shelter on Burnside in the Old Town district.

Old Town, the part of Portland formerly known as the North End, has always been a gathering place for a transient population. Before World War II, the economy of the Pacific Northwest depended on a large population of transient workers to fill seasonal agricultural, timber, and mining jobs. By the 1950s, the economy had changed significantly, and the demand for migrant workers decreased. The North End, along with the Tenderloin and S.E. Grand Avenue, became known as "skid row" where aging working men lived in rooming houses and single-room occupancy (SRO) hotels among a growing population of unemployable and troubled workers.

Decades of rising property values, "urban renewal," and economic recession changed the neighborhood further, and by 1991, Old Town was the epicenter of a large population of destitute people, mostly men, with nowhere to live. A more-or-less permanent class of "homeless" gathered in the shelters near Burnside Street, and hundreds of people slept on the streets and in doorways every night. Among the homeless on that cold night in October were Tony Nelson, out of work for months, and an ex-convict and unsuccessful conman named Randy Scott Henry (a.k.a. Marty McDaniel). Nelson and Henry must have seen opportunity when the man in the old Toyota showed up at the mission with promises of work clearing land outside of Portland. Bill Cash, another homeless man,

Douglas Franklin Wright always did well when he was in prison. It was only when he was free that he was dangerous. (*Multnomah County Library*)

who worked part-time at the mission, recognized the man in the Toyota as Douglas Franklin Wright. Wright had been hanging around the shelter for weeks, offering work to desperate men and taking them away. Cash was among the few who realized that the men who left with Wright never seemed to return.

Douglas Franklin Wright, born in Iowa in 1940, spent most of his life in institutions of one kind or another. After his parents' divorce, Wright moved with his mother to California where, at the age of seventeen, he was convicted of molesting a five-year-old boy in 1957. Most of Wright's sentence was served at Atascadero State Hospital near San Luis Obispo. Atascadero, opened in 1953 to confine and treat sex offenders, earned the nickname "Dachau for gays" from its aggressive "homosexual conversion" treatments. Released in 1959, Wright moved north to Portland where he connected with a gang of burglars run by Richard Sheldon Clifford.

Clifford, a life-long criminal who was on parole when he died in 2006 at the age of seventy, had a lot in common with members of the Broadway Gang, the juvenile burglars and robbers who hung out on S.W. Broadway near the original Lincoln High School.[1] Starting at the age of seventeen in 1953, Clifford was arrested repeatedly on suspicion of burglary and assault. By 1960, he was running a gang of young criminals who committed burglaries all over Portland and as far away as Boise, Bend, and Eugene. Using the pool room at Amato's Bowling Lanes in southeast Portland as headquarters, Clifford insulated himself from prosecution and exercised brutal discipline on his gang if they failed to obey or went against him in any way.

Douglas Wright fit in well. His large, imposing physical presence made him a natural enforcer for Clifford's will; his low intelligence made him a loyal follower. He was arrested several times between 1959 and 1961, but only on suspicion of various crimes and he did not face serious jail time until he was convicted for a grocery store burglary in 1962. The conviction resulted in a six-year term in the Oregon State Penitentiary.

After years in the harsh environment of the Atascadero State Hospital, Wright found the Oregon State Penitentiary a comfortable place. Popular among the other prisoners, Wright became a competitive weight-lifter and earned his nickname, "the Animal." For the next thirty years, with only brief periods of freedom, the state prison in Salem would be Douglas Wright's most frequented home.

Released in June 1968, Wright returned to Portland, where he received a warm welcome from Richard Clifford. Clifford's burglary ring was at the height of its power by 1968 and Clifford had become paranoid protecting his interests. Conflict with a rival burglary ring in Eugene led to the murder of Paul DeGeorge in October 1968. DeGeorge's death seems to have come out of a Machiavellian plot against the burglary ring run by Richard Clifford's rival, Donnie Ray Gardner. Dennis Melvin Goodin, the man who was eventually convicted of DeGeorge's murder on Gardner's order, was probably working for Clifford and was most likely responsible for the burglary of Gardner's home that DeGeorge was blamed for. After killing DeGeorge near Marcola, in Lane County, Goodin fled to Portland where he hid out, under Clifford's protection, and teamed up with the Animal for a series of grocery store burglaries.

In June 1969, Wright and Goodin were captured inside the Foster Food Market in southeast Portland. They had cut their way into the store through the roof and surrendered after the police surrounded the building. Goodin was identified from his fingerprints as a fugitive from Lane County. Before he could be tried on the burglary charge Wright, released on bail, would be involved with the first spectacular crime of his career and he would become the object of Multnomah County's largest manhunt to date.

It stemmed from a conflict between Richard Clifford and a member of the robbery gang, Kenneth Snelling. Snelling, who served four years in the Oregon Correctional Institute for burglary and escape, was a longtime friend of Gerald Rapue, who along with his brother, Ken, had been a member of Clifford's gang for a decade. Released from OCI around the same time Douglas Wright was released from O.S.P., Snelling returned to Portland and went back to work for Clifford. In December 1968, he married a divorced mother of a young boy, Gail Kaarhus. Clifford never trusted Snelling's wife, who fenced the burglary ring's product. Soon, he came to believe that Gail was working undercover for the police.

If Gail Snelling was working for the police, it is a secret the bureau has kept for fifty years. It is more likely that Clifford's suspicions came from his growing paranoia. The gang was becoming more violent and "trigger happy" by this point, most likely influenced by the fearful Clifford. Besides the 1968 murder in Eugene, there was a June 1969 assault in which Ken Rapue, a longtime gang member, fired a pistol at three teenage girls on a southeast Portland street. In October 1969, Rapue fired the weapon that killed Glenn Ennen, a Bend tavern owner who surprised the Rapue brothers and two accomplices as they robbed his bar.

Tensions between Clifford and Snelling came to a head during a confrontation at the Red Garter Tavern on S.E. 92nd Avenue on August 3, 1969. The argument turned physical, and Snelling was badly beaten before Clifford left the tavern. A couple of hours later, after recovering from the initial trauma of the beating, Snelling went to a nearby

In 1959, Amato's Supper Club closed downtown and reopened the next year as a bowling alley and restaurant on the east side. Amato's Bowling Lanes was the unofficial headquarters of Richard Clifford's robbery gang. (*Oregon Historical Society*)

house on S.E. Insley Street, looking for Clifford. Clifford was waiting for him and soon put a bullet in Snelling's belly.

The bullet paralyzed Snelling from the waist down, but it did not resolve the conflict or Clifford's suspicions about Gail. Gail Snelling and her mother, Margaret Rosenberry, who shared the house with her, began receiving phone calls threatening them. "Shut your mouth or get your head blown off," was the most descriptive of the threats. With her husband still hospitalized, Gail went to a local private detective, Robert Hayes, on September 1 to ask for protection. That very night, about 1.30 a.m., the Animal showed up at the family's northeast Portland home.

Matsen "Matt" Kaarhus, Gail Snelling's five-year-old son, told a compelling story at Wright's 1970 trial. His mother was away from home that night and he stayed up late in the care of his grandmother. Matt woke up in the middle of the night because he could hear his grandmother arguing with somebody. He went to her room and found her with the man he called Doug. Margaret told the boy to go back to bed and he did, not waking up again until about 7.30 the next morning. Shortly after Matt returned to bed, Douglas Wright fired three bullets into Margaret Rosenberry's head, covering her corpse with blankets perhaps so the boy would not see her, or possibly, like many killers after the fact, he felt remorse for what he had done.

As the boy presumably slept, Wright ransacked the house, discovering a .45 pistol, and then paced for some time, smoking cigarettes while he waited for Gail Snelling to return home. During his 1994 trial for the Warm Springs killings, Wright confessed to a handgun fetish based on his enjoyment of the fear on his victims' faces when they saw his gun pointed at them. His fetish for handguns and his love of killing may have originated on the morning of September 2, 1969, when Gail Snelling arrived home just before 7.30 a.m. Confronting the young mother at the front door, Wright threatened her with the .45 before firing a bullet into her face. While she was on her knees in the foyer, he fired another shot into the back of her head to make sure she was dead. Covering her body with blanket, Wright woke the frightened boy, gathered him up, and took him away.

The double murder in the quiet suburban neighborhood was not discovered until after 9 a.m. and by then, Wright and young Matt Kaarhus had effectively disappeared. The missing boy prompted a manhunt unprecedented in Portland history. Shortly after the killing, Wright's car—a green Oldsmobile—was stopped by a traffic cop, but the alert had not yet gone out on the little boy and the cop let Wright go with a warning. Wright decided to get off the street and checked into the Ninety-Nine W Motel on S.W. Barbur Blvd. Wright and Kaarhus stayed together at the motel for two days before Wright abandoned the boy. No one knows, except Matt Kaarhus, what he went through in those two days, but Wright's sexual obsession with young boys, often a symptom of childhood sexual abuse, is well-documented, so sexual assault likely occurred. Two

The double murder and abduction of a young boy led to the largest manhunt Portland had experienced up to that time. (*Multnomah County Library*)

days later, one of the other motel guests realized that the five-year-old boy was on his own and called the police, ending a search that involved law enforcement agencies from eleven states.

Richard Clifford and several members of his gang were arrested as material witnesses in the double murder, and it did not take long for the police to issue a warrant for Douglas Wright's arrest. Clifford may have been the obvious suspect, but his well-organized gang had good resources for protection. Wright hunkered down in a maintenance shed near the Pumpkin Ridge Golf Course and remained free for weeks as the police searched for him. He must have been bored and feeling pretty safe more than a month later, on October 18, when he and Arthur Tibbets visited Banks Billiards in the small town of Banks, in western Washington County. After drinking and playing pool, Tibbets got into an argument with Donald Tennyson as he and Wright were leaving. The argument turned into a fight in the parking lot, and Tibbets got the worst of it with a broken jaw. Wright fired four shots at Tibbets' attacker, striking him once in the arm, and the two men jumped into Tibbets' car and fled.

Wright, who was using the alias Gary Wattenberg, was recognized right away and the manhunt focused on Washington County. Shortly before midnight on October 21, Washington County Sheriff's Sergeant Stan Friese was searching the Pumpkin Ridge Golf Course looking for Wright when someone called in the report of a suspicious person walking along S.W. 272nd Avenue north of Hillsboro. Traffic was heavy along the rural road, and Friese recognized Wright immediately as he drove up behind the fugitive. Friese got the drop on Wright, ordered him to surrender, and made him lie down on the ground, spread eagle, but at that point, they reached a standoff. Friese knew he was dealing with a dangerous fugitive who was probably armed. Being by himself, he could not leave Wright alone to return to his car and call for help, but neither could he take the gun off his prisoner long enough to search him. As Sheriff Warren Barnes told *The Oregonian*, "The officer didn't dare move."

A passing motorist, Harold L. Viesenback, Jr., came to Sgt. Friese's rescue. Viesenback held Friese's gun on Wright, while the deputy searched him. Friese found two .38 caliber handguns, ninety rounds of ammunition, and a long knife concealed in Wright's clothes.[2] As violent as Douglas Wright could be when he was free, once he was under arrest, he was docile and submissive, like many life-long criminals, content with the structure of prison life. In a jail cell, Wright seemed to feel safe, and he was always polite and cooperative with his guards. Before he was charged in the murders of Gail Snelling and Margaret Rosenberry, Wright was sentenced to ten years for shooting Donald Tennyson in Banks.

On the same day that Wright was arrested in Washington County, closing arguments began in the trial of his friend Dennis Goodin for the murder of Paul DeGeorge in Eugene. Goodin's trial lasted more than seven weeks and heard testimony from a staggering eighty-three witnesses. It was the longest jury trial Lane County had seen up to that time, and Goodin was convicted on October 24 of murder. Although Richard Clifford was never charged in DeGeorge's murder, he faced an attempted murder charge in Multnomah County for shooting Ken Snelling in August. After Gerald and Ken Rapue lied on the witness stand, Clifford was acquitted on December 17. Wright seemed content back in the Oregon State Prison, where he whiled away the time with old friends like Dennis Goodin and new friends like Gary Gilmore and Vincent Capitan.

On June 9, 1970, Douglas Wright was arrested in his prison cell for two counts of first-degree murder—Gail Snelling and Margaret Rosenberry—and one count of kidnapping—young Matsen Kaarhus. Richard Clifford was arrested at his girlfriend's house in S.E. Portland on the same charges that day as well.

The year 1970 was an important one for Assistant District Attorney Desmond "Des" Connall. He gained broad public attention with two trials in 1969: railroading the Jorgenson brothers in the Peyton-Allen case and, convicting Vincent "The Iceman" Capitan for the murder of Carlos Mendoza.[3] As he prepared to take Douglas Franklin Wright and Richard Sheldon Clifford to trial, Connall was also preparing for his promotion to district attorney. When Douglas Wright's trial opened in November 1970, Connall played up the "gangland" and "over-arching conspiracy" aspects of the case. The gambit paid off for Connall in publicity, and *The Oregonian* provided breathless coverage of the dramatic trial. It did not hurt that George DesBrisay, the popular defense attorney and ex-longshoreman who would become one of the city's most important drug importers in the next decade, represented Wright's defense.

There was plenty of evidence of conspiracy to go around. While giving testimony in the case, Gerald Rapue inadvertently admitted that he was working on Richard Clifford's orders when he broke into the M&J Tavern in Bend, where he stole nearly $1,000 in rolled coins. During that robbery, tavern owner Glenn Ennen surprised the robbers and Ken Rapue shot him to death. Another murder charge was added to Richard Clifford's growing docket. There was drama, too. Neighbors described the peaceful morning, which happened to be the first day of school, in the quiet suburban neighborhood. The peace was broken, they said, by the sound of gunshots and a car speeding away.

Then six-year-old Matt Kaarhus, the "tow-headed blond" boy with the "perfect smile" and all-American good looks, took the stand. The courtroom was cleared during the boy's testimony and *The Oregonian* was noticeably discrete in what it printed. Matt was "nervous" on the stand, but he and Wright smiled at each other "affectionately" as the boy identified "Doug." After gentle questioning, the boy revealed that he had "looked under one of the blankets" that covered the bloody corpses of his mother and his grandmother. After the boy's wrenching testimony, the court recessed for the weekend, early so Des Connall could drive to Salem and be sworn in by Governor Tom McCall as the new Multnomah County district attorney.

Little Matt's testimony was powerful and made a deep impression on all who witnessed it. After intense negotiations over the weekend between Connall and DesBrisay, Douglas Wright pled guilty to two counts of second-degree murder and was sentenced to two consecutive terms of twenty-five years each, the first one to begin only after he completed the ten-year sentence for assault with a deadly weapon he was currently serving. The kidnapping charge and the burglary charge with Dennis Goodin were dropped, and Multnomah County agreed not to bring any other charges against Wright that might come up in their continuing investigation of Clifford's operation. It was a good deal for everyone. Wright was happy in prison, and it saved Multnomah County as much as $25,000 ($160,000 today) in court costs. Circuit Judge Alfred T. Sulmonetti explained to the jury as he dismissed them, "Because of Wright's record he probably would spend the rest of his years in prison."

The Oregon State Penitentiary was full of charismatic, dominant men in 1970. Carl Bowles, Gary Gilmore, Stephen Kessler, Vincent Capitan, and now Richard Clifford, who had been convicted as an accessory in the Snelling and Rosenberry murders, each with his own followers, controlled the prison underworld. The Animal, with his slow, plodding mind and muscular body, was a natural follower. In the aftermath of the fiery 1968 riot, the Oregon State Prison was changing rapidly. The new warden, Hoyt Cupp, who had been a guard for more than twenty years, instituted many changes to improve conditions and morale, but as he told *The Oregonian,* "The young prisoners are aggressive. They feel they have been treated unfairly. They will grasp any opportunity to show ugliness."

One opportunity came on February 6, 1971, when more than 120 prisoners in the segregation unit, where infractions were punished, staged a "sit-down" strike. *The Oregonian* did not report the reasons for the prisoners' strike, but there were many complaints about the use of solitary confinement to punish even mundane rule infractions. Things settled down after the strike, but a few days later thirty prisoners in segregation set fire to their mattresses and tore up the toilets in their cells. In a spasm of frustration, the prisoners did more than $12,000 ($75,000 today) damage to the prison, even burning their own uniforms and leaving more than fifty prisoners naked. Four prisoners, singled out as ring-leaders, were transferred to federal prisons for their part in the riot; among them were Gary Gilmore, who went to the new maximum-security unit at Marion, IL, and, Douglas Franklin Wright, who went to Leavenworth.[4]

Wright exhibited good behavior at Leavenworth and was soon back home in Salem. Warden Cupp had expanded educational opportunities at the prison in an effort to improve prisoner morale and prepare them for life on the outside. Although judges were giving longer sentences for violent crimes, Cupp was aware that most prisoners, even the most violent, would not serve their full terms. In 1977, Wright became the first inmate to complete an apprenticeship program when he became a journeyman upholsterer. Wright enthused about the prospect of opening his own business in Portland, saying, "That was part of my problem before. I didn't know what I wanted to do." Although Wright was scheduled to remain in prison until at least 2004, Kent Ward, the director of the prison's apprenticeship program, thought he had a good chance to be released at his next parole hearing in 1985. In 1982, Wright received conditional release so he could enroll at Western Oregon University in Monmouth, where he completed a Bachelor's degree in sociology.

On May 23, 1984, Luke Treadway, a ten-year-old boy who had struggled with poor health for most of his short life, disappeared as he walked from his mother's house in southeast Portland to the home of a friend from school. No one suspected the ex-convict, ex-mental patient with a record of molesting young boys who now lived in their neighborhood. No one suspected that a new serial killer had been born. Douglas Wright, who had given up on his "dream" of opening a one-man upholstery shop, worked as a landscaper and fulfilled his parole obligations, but the stress was starting to show and his lack of impulse control would soon be obvious. Two months later, on July 28, Wright drove up to a group of three men standing in the parking lot of the Safeway store on S.E. Woodstock. Pointing a gun into the face of one of the men, Wright said, "I won't hurt you, but if I have to, I'll kill you."

He forced the three men to accompany him into the store where he confronted the assistant manager, demanding he open the safe. When the manager fumbled the combination the first time, Wright said, "Hurry up. If the cops get here before I'm gone,

I'll kill somebody." Wright filled a plastic garbage bag with cash from the safe and the store's tills, firing one shot before he left. As he drove away, a witness took down his license plate number and Wright was promptly arrested the next morning. It may have been the second time Wright robbed that particular Safeway; after his arrest, he was charged with the April 26 robbery of the same store, but there was not enough evidence to convict him. After not quite two years of freedom, Wright was back home in the Oregon State Penitentiary, where he likely felt safer and Portland was definitely safer with him confined.

At the age of forty-four, Douglas Wright had spent more than half his life behind bars in Salem. He had proven time and again that he was a violent criminal who was not safe outside incarceration, but as he was such a "model prisoner," he was released again in June 1991. He took an apartment in Tigard, bought a used Toyota, and again went to work as a landscaper.

Serial killers, who kill three or more victims in separate, repeated incidents, have been with us since the earliest times, but in the 1970s and 1980s, their crimes were recognized and classified. From Ted Bundy through the Green River Killer and the Molalla Forest Killer, the Pacific Northwest has seen more than its share of serial killers. Many of them have lived and killed in Portland. By 1991, serial killing was almost a popular crime, glamorized in movies and books. Serial killers claim to have different motives for engaging their violent impulses, but the unvarnished truth is they like to kill. They enjoy it and in time they become addicted to murder.

Douglas Franklin Wright later claimed that he had developed a hatred of homeless people while he was in prison. The truth is the homeless men in Old Town were simply vulnerable and easy targets. Each easily seduced with promises of outdoor work and good pay, and with no one to care or look for them if they disappeared.

On October 4, 1991, Wright picked up Anthony Arthur Baker, a fugitive from a California prison, near the Greyhound Bus Station in northwest Portland. He drove him to the Warm Springs Indian Reservation, where he shot and killed him before burying him in the desert. It was the third occasion on which Wright had kidnapped a man from Old Town; later, the police found the bodies of William Clement Marks and William Ray Davis buried in the vicinity of Baker's corpse.

Three weeks later, on October 22, Wright picked up Tony Nelson and Marty McDaniel at the Recovery Inn with promises of work and brighter days. They drove to the Warm Springs Reservation. McDaniel, who survived the trip, told a harrowing story. When they arrived at the remote location, Wright took Nelson away from the car and shot him in the face. He returned for McDaniel, but the frightened young man escaped and ran, barefoot, into the desert. Flagging down a car, McDaniel hitched a ride and told the driver about what had just happened. The driver, Ervie Dominguez, identified himself as an off-duty tribal policeman and stopped to call authorities. McDaniel, completely panicked by now, jumped out of the car and ran away, making his way back to Portland. The next day, when Portland police tracked McDaniel down at the mission, Bill Cash identified the driver of the Toyota as Douglas Franklin Wright.

Convicted on federal firearms charges, Wright was held in Oregon while the serial killing investigation was underway. Since Tony Nelson was a member of the Makah tribe and killed on Indian land, his murder was a federal crime, which had no death penalty at the time; Wright was never tried for Nelson's murder. In 1994, Wasco County

The Oregon State Prison, the place where Douglas Wright lived for nearly thirty years. (*Oregon Historical Society*)

convicted him of the murders of Anthony Baker, William Marks, and William Davis and sentenced Wright to death.

Capital punishment has always been a controversial topic in Oregon. In 1914, voters banned the death penalty by initiative, but six years later, another initiative overwhelmingly reinstated capital punishment. In 1964, Measure 1 passed with more than 60 percent of the vote, once again outlawing capital punishment in Oregon. In 1978 and 1984, new measure reinstated the death penalty, but the issue was challenged in court and no one faced execution in the state until Douglas Franklin Wright's execution in 1996. He became the first man in Oregon executed by lethal injection.

Like his friend Gary Gilmore, executed in Utah in 1977, Wright refused to appeal his death sentence. In a sense he forced Gov. John Kitzhaber, a strong opponent of capital punishment, to kill him.[5] During his last days, Wright showed signs that he was trying to tie up the loose ends of his life. He confessed to the murder of Luke Treadway, which he had never been suspected of, and tried unsuccessfully to lead the police to the boy's body, buried near his other victims on the Warm Springs Reservation. In addition, he wrote a letter to the people of the Warm Springs Nations apologizing for the stain he left by burying his victims on their land. He said it was a mistake because he thought he was in the Mount Hood National Forest, and he hoped that his death would atone for his crimes and erase the stigma he had left on their land.

13

THE FORGOTTEN
SERIAL KILLER

*He was a predator, nothing less. What's worse is that he lived in my neighborhood
and I was afraid for my family while he was loose.*

Det. Mike Hefley

Although her life had been difficult, raising two little boys on her own, Norene Davis
was a cheerful person, very popular with her customers at The General Store where she
worked as a waitress. Norene loved country music, and she often danced as she made
her way from table to table, her trademark cowboy hat perched on her head during the
late-night shifts she worked at the popular Metzger-area nightspot, which featured live
music and nude dancing. She was not one of the nude performers—she waited tables—
but she was so popular among her regular customers and fellow-employees they all
called her "Happy." Norene was quiet about her private life, rarely talking about her
ex-husband who abandoned her in 1978 with one infant son and pregnant with another.
She was also quiet about her friends. Her two roommates, who also worked at The
General Store, thought she was dating a man with the surname Brown who repaired the
lawnmower for them, but they had never met him. When the emergency phone call came
shortly before the end of her shift, it was not unusual that Norene identified the caller
only as "a friend who had an emergency but couldn't go to the police."

Norene grew up in the small town of Rupert, ID, where she graduated from Minico
High School, showing talent as a singer. Like many who grew up in the vast desert of
central Idaho, she married early and moved away soon. She, her husband, and a sister,
Verdene Fairchild, settled in West Linn, OR. Norene found work at the G.A.F. factory
in Progress, where she made Viewmaster slide-viewing devices, and started working
part-time as a waitress. Her husband left in 1978, and though they never filed for
divorce, she never saw him again. In January 1980, Norene was laid-off from her job at
G.A.F. and she started working full-time as a late-night waitress at The General Store.

Evicted from her Gladstone apartment, Norene moved with her two young sons to
her sister's place and in January 1981, she was able to rent a small house in Aloha with
two other waitresses sharing expenses. With food-stamps and tips, Norene eked out an

Alvin "Bud" Brown after his 1991 arrest.
(*Private Collection*)

existence for her family and she always tried to make the best of things. She was known as a loyal friend who could be counted on for help, so no one thought anything of it when she left work at 3 a.m. on Monday, May 18, 1981, to help a friend in need.

Norene Davis did not come home that morning. About 12.30 p.m. the Washington County Sheriff's Office received a report of a car abandoned on S.W. 93rd Avenue near Macdonald Street. Norene's car was left alongside the road, headlights on, out of gas, but with the ignition still switched on. Her purse with tips inside sat on the front seat. The car had been there, a five-minute drive from The General Store in the opposite direction from Norene's home in Aloha, since early in the morning. The sheriff's deputy who responded to the call was puzzled; there were no signs of a struggle. It was as if the driver pulled off the road, stepped out of the car, and just disappeared.

The car was at the top of a steep overgrown ravine. After about thirty minutes of searching, the deputy found Norene's body, wrapped in a bloodstained blanket, near the bottom of the gulley. She had been thrown down the steep hill, strangled, and stabbed repeatedly. Robin Chicks, one of Norene's roommates, said the hardest part about Norene Davis' brutal death was finding the words to tell her two sons, aged four and five, that their mother was never coming home. "I just said that for reasons we couldn't understand, the Lord decided that he could use her better in heaven than we could on Earth," she told *Oregonian* reporter Benny Evangelista, Jr.

The brutal crime shocked quiet Washington County and became one of the county's few unsolved homicide cases. Only a few blocks away in a working-class neighborhood in Portland's farthest southwest corner, shocking crimes had become routine and the citizens lived in fear, especially the women. The quiet suburban neighborhood was served by Jackson High School and Portland Community College's nearby Sylvania Campus. Neighborhood kids walked to school and thought nothing of a ten- or twenty-block walk to visit friends, but now, hand-lettered signs decorated the telephone poles along

S.W. Taylors Ferry Road and the surrounding neighborhood. "Walk in Safety," one read. "Be Cautious," read another. "Be on Guard," read a third, "Rapist Around!"

The southwest Portland neighborhood had originally been rural housing for workers on the interurban streetcar lines that networked Oregon at the turn of the twentieth century; by the 1980s, the neighborhood of rolling hills and large yards had become a bedroom community for the industry of nearby Washington County. The children of the baby boomer generation were nearing adulthood, and they thought nothing of long walks on streets with no sidewalks. Adolescent women walking near the campuses of Jackson High and Portland Community College, Sylvania had begun to fall prey to violent attacks.

Nancy Logan, a sophomore at Jackson High in 1981, remembers it very well, "Because my part of the story ended positively—him in jail, me alive—I am very comfortable talking about it." Eighteen-year-old Kim Stevens, a senior at Jackson preparing to transfer to P.C.C., was friends with Nancy's older brother. Kim's fourteen-year-old sister was a close friend of Nancy's. Less than a block away lived an elderly couple, Alvin and Christine Brown, and their two grandsons, Steve "Stick" and Alvin "Bud." The Brown family had come under pressure because of the behavior of their oldest grandson, Bud.

Portland Detective Cordes Towle, who attended Markham Elementary School in seventh and eighth grades with Stick Brown, remembers Stick's older brother, who was two grades ahead, as an awe-inspiring figure. Towle went to Benson High School instead of Jackson, where Stick and Bud went, as did Nancy Logan and Kim Stevens, eight years later. Still a car enthusiast, Towle remembers cruising "the gut" (along S.W. Broadway) and stopping for gas where Barbur Boulevard ends at Highway 99, near Tigard. The gas station there was a hangout for teenage car buffs and Stick and Bud, in

Portland International Raceway in North Portland was a frequent destination for car buff Bud Brown. (*Portland City Archive*)

their restored classic cars (a candy-apple red 1957 Chevy and a "cherry" 1968 Chevy Nova, respectively) were regular visitors. Towle also attended racing meets together with the Browns at Portland International Raceway, while they were in High School.

Bud graduated from Jackson High School in 1973, but he continued to live with his grandparents on S.W. 61st Ave, supporting himself with mechanic and landscaping jobs. His loud car and fast driving became a neighborhood hazard, and Bud himself was a regular sight, working on his car or standing in the driveway, ogling teenage girls as they walked by. Neighbors who tried to talk to Bud were confronted with a cold, intimidating stare or Bud's hot temper, and they found it was not worth the trouble to say anything. Eight years after graduation, little had changed, but Bud had grown bolder.

Early in April 1981, fifteen-year-old Nancy Logan was attacked and raped as she walked along S.W. Taylor's Ferry Road. She recognized Bud as her attacker and he was quickly arrested, charged with rape. That was when the first signs went up. Brown's family responded to accusations against Bud with a sign reading, "Thou shalt not bear false witness against your neighbor." The neighborhood, convinced that Bud was dangerous, responded with its own signs. Logan remembers that feeling ran high in the polarized neighborhood, and her mother had emotional confrontations with the high school principal as she organized self-defense classes and neighborhood meetings. Bud Brown was only held for a few days and then released on bail with a trial scheduled in August.

A few days after Brown's release, Melina Crist, a seventeen-year-old freshman at Portland Community College, did not come home after school. Police searched the wooded area around the Sylvania campus, where her mother dropped her off for class on May 5, but they found no trace of the young woman. Four days later, seventeen-year-old Kimberly Stevens was walking along S.W. 62nd Avenue on her way to her boyfriend's house on a Friday evening. After she passed the Southwood Park First Evangelical Church, she came to a patch of trees. As she passed a steep ravine leading into the woods, someone grabbed her and threw her into the bushes. Before she could recover her breath from the fall, the man was on top of her. The next morning, Kim's father realized that the usually responsible young woman had never come home.

Two missing teenagers and one brutally raped in less than sixty days raised tension in the neighborhood. More warning signs went up, "No More Rape!" Kim Stevens' body, strangled to death and partially clothed, was found on Sunday. On Monday, Noreen Davis was found strangled and stabbed just blocks away in Tigard, again thrown down a hill. Women finally became emboldened by what *Oregonian* reporter Tom Hallman, Jr., called a protest against rape. They began to come forward with stories of bizarre and frightening experiences. In February, one woman received a phone call from a man who said her son had been in a serious accident. The man asked her to pick him up at a designated spot and he would take her to the scene. She picked him up, and after driving a few miles, he confessed that there had been no accident, but that he was going to rape her. She put up a fight and ran from the car but kept the whole thing secret for months. Another woman said that in March, she received a similar phone call, but when she got to the spot, she could see there was no accident and became suspicious. She sped away and was relieved to find there had been no accident.

People in Portland were scared, especially women. Gun sales rose as fearful neighbors armed themselves. Women stopped going out after dark or walking by themselves.

On May 29, another Friday night, Sheila Burnett, a popular "Avon Lady" who sold cosmetics to most of the women in the same southwest neighborhood, got a disturbing phone call while she was home alone. The excited voice on the call was familiar, the grandson of one of her clients. His garbled voice, distorted by excitement, said her son had been in an accident and was on his way to Providence Hospital. Sheila's son, a recent graduate of Jackson High, had taken a job out of town, but fear clouded Sheila's mind. The familiar voice said, "I'll pick you up. Drive you to the hospital." Sheila Burnett, the daughter of Vernon Garrick, one of southeast Portland's pioneer realtors, now a fifty-seven-year-old mother of teenagers, left a note for her husband and disappeared.

Portland Detective Mike Hefley, promoted to the homicide squad in 1981, remembers the Kimberly Stevens case as his first murder investigation. With a crime scene just blocks from the detective's own home and no evidence to connect the man who was palpably guilty to his crime the case remained officially unsolved. Fear kept a firm grip on the neighborhood, and Bud Brown reveled in it. Hefley remembers Brown standing in his driveway in front of his house, head raised, nostrils flared as if sniffing for the scent of prey, daring him to make a move against him. The ability to intimidate people was a power Bud Brown possessed, and most of the police officers who arrested him over the years expressed fear of him when they told of the experience years later.

Hefley would have good reason to remember every encounter he had with Bud Brown over the next two decades as he became a well-known homicide detective, investigating some of Portland's most important cases, including Mulegeta Seraw's murder in 1988 and the convoluted Charbonneau case in 1992.[1] Kim Stevens' murder remained unsolved until the twenty-first century when DNA evidence became advanced enough to finally prove it was Bud Brown who killed her. By then, Brown was spending his last days in the Oregon State Penitentiary for another crime, but Hefley, along with Washington County detective Paul Lazenby, who finally solved Norene Davis' murder with DNA evidence, felt compelled to make sure he would never be released again.

In addition to troubling his neighbors, Bud was also a regular hazard of the bars along S.W. Barbur Boulevard. A loud, belligerent drunk known for sexually harassing women and "gay bashing," Bud was lucky not to come to the attention of the police sooner than he did. In one memorable incident at the Pink Pearl Tavern, Bud sexually harassed Portland Police Officer Terry Wagner at the bar. Wagner, one of the first uniformed women police officers in Portland, often stopped at the Pink Pearl for coffee during her shift. On this particular occasion, Bud, visibly intoxicated, accosted her as she sat at the bar, telling her that women could not make good cops. Wagner felt threatened, but Bud's brother, Stick, dragged him away before she could arrest him.

It was not until 1979 that Bud had his first real trouble with the law. In May, Officer Steve Coffman was working on a prostitution investigation at a tavern called Fred's Place on N.E. Union Avenue (now Martin Luther King Jr. Boulevard). He had been watching the place for days, observing a young woman named Adele Asher (not her real name), who had eleven arrests for prostitution and was openly soliciting near the tavern's front door. So far, he had not seen her successfully pick up any tricks, but on the 12th, he watched as a gold-colored 1965 Mercury Station Wagon passed by Fred's Place and then came around the block to make contact with Asher, who climbed into the car.

Coffman followed the station wagon to the parking garage at Lloyd Center, not far away. He kept the car under surveillance as it took a parking spot, the driver leaned back, and Asher's head ducked down toward the seat. It was a routine prostitution arrest, except for the fact that Bud Brown would not cooperate. Coffman got a good look at what the woman was doing, and he got a clear view of Brown's face as he approached the car with his badge in his hand. The occupants of the car were startled when Coffman knocked on the closed window and ordered them out. "No, I won't," Bud yelled through the window and backed the car out of the parking space at high speed. Coffman had to jump back to avoid being hit as the car tore out of the parking lot, tires squealing. Bud got away, but Officer Coffman, who did not bother to pursue, would never forget him.

Coffman went back to watching Fred's Place, which was located in a neighborhood designated a "high vice area." Asher did not show up again until May 15, and she refused to cooperate, claiming she had been at Laurelhurst Park all night on the 12th. On May 17, the gold Mercury was stopped on N.E. Union, not far from Fred's Place. Bud Brown was driving, and Coffman recognized him as the driver who almost hit him on the 12th. Coffman asked Brown if he had ever seen him before, but Brown denied it. Asked about the incident on May 12, Brown claimed he had been at a stag party that evening. Brown produced a driver's license that had been suspended for failure to appear in court for traffic tickets. A search of the station wagon found less than an ounce of marijuana and the list of charges against Brown was long—driving with a suspended license; misuse of a driver's license; reckless endangerment (which Coffman wanted to change to Assault with a Dangerous Weapon); and possession of less than an ounce of marijuana.

No information is available on the outcome of the 1979 charges against Brown. It is likely he paid a fine and the charges were dropped. That would not be the case in 1981. In August, he was convicted of one charge of rape and one charge of sodomy in the April 3 attack on Nancy Logan. Tension in the southwest Portland neighborhood eased somewhat after the spasm of violence in May, but people still reported getting phone calls about family members in accidents. They had become suspicious of the telephone trick, though. The middle-aged mother of Chuck Luce, a friend of Cordes Towle who attended middle school with Stick Brown, got a call that summer about an accident her son had supposedly been in. She took her husband and daughter with her and drove to the remote location where the "accident" had occurred. There was no accident, but a man stood beside his car on the side of the road and the family drove away. The phone calls stopped after Bud was sentenced to two consecutive twenty-year terms in prison on October 2, 1981.

The neighborhood breathed a little easier with Bud Brown in jail, but the more Mike Hefley learned about Kim Stevens, the less he could let go of the murder case. He was convinced that Brown was the killer, but he had only circumstantial evidence to connect him to the crime. A white car closely matching the description of Brown's battered Oldsmobile had been seen cruising the neighborhood and sitting outside the Stevens house the day of the murder. The effect of the murder on Stevens' traumatized family— her father Victor B. Stevens and two young sisters—made Hefley more determined than ever to convict her killer, but there was little he could do. In November 1983, construction workers at a vacant lot on S.W. Barbur Boulevard unearthed the skeleton of Melina Crist, the seventeen-year-old P.C.C. student who went missing shortly before Kim Stevens' murder. The girl had been strangled, but her body was too badly decomposed to tell much else.

Bud Brown was a frequent customer of prostitutes on Union Ave. They later became his victims. (*Oregon Historical Society*)

The complicated "matrix system," which calculated how much of his sentence a convict had to serve—a system that was called "a fraud on the public"—meant Bud would not have to be in prison long, even with two twenty-year sentences. In less than four years, he was out on parole, and by 1986, Brown was a free man again. He moved in with his grandparents yet again and got a new landscaping job. The elder Alvin Brown had been diagnosed with Alzheimer's disease, and Bud, unsurprisingly, became interested in the young in-home healthcare worker who cared for his grandfather, a young woman named Jackie Haratyk.

Bud was still a man filled with rage against women, but he was learning to effectively conceal it from the people in his life, except in specific cases. Bud did not like cops, and he acted out in every encounter he had with them. Robert King, who later had a long career in the Portland police bureau, remembers an encounter with Bud in 1986, while he was a rookie and still working with a coach on the Lake Oswego Police Force.

Bud, who was living in Lake Oswego at the time, had just finished probation after his release from the Oregon State Penitentiary. He failed to appear in court for a hearing on a drunken driving arrest, and Robert King, accompanied by his police coach, served him with a failure to appear warrant at his home. After an intense stand-off over whether he could brush his teeth before being taken into custody (a confrontation that Bud won), he surprised the rookie cop by meekly submitting to arrest. In the car on the way to the station, though, something changed; Bud became threatening, promising that he would find out where King lived and come there to kill him. Unnerved, King who lived in southeast Portland, alerted the police bureau and had his house "flagged" so patrolling officers would keep an eye on the place and be aware of the threats that had been made. "Alvin Brown is the single most evil guy I've run across in twenty-four years as a police officer," King observed.

Bud claimed that all the attention he got from the police over the years was unfair prejudice and happened because he was an ex-con. Officers like Mike Hefley, Cordes Towle, Terry Wagner, Robert King, and Paul Lazenby felt it was the danger he posed to society and women in particular that caught their attention. In 1987, Cordes Towle remembers getting a "courtesy report" from Washington County about a Tigard woman's frightening experience. She was waiting at a bus stop when a pickup truck screeched to a halt. A powerful man came out of the truck, picked her up, and bodily put her into the passenger seat. He said his name was Bud and he drove her around for hours, holding down the electric door locks. He injected cocaine in front of her several times and tried to convince her to have sex with him. She escaped when he stopped for gas, scrambling from the truck and running away. She reported that the pickup had a frame on the back and the logo of a landscaping company on the door. Towle, the childhood friend of Bud's estranged brother, felt a chill as he read the report. He drove by the Brown house on S.W. 61st and saw Bud's pickup truck in the driveway, a metal frame on the back and the logo of a landscaping company on the door. The woman could not identify Bud Brown from a photo line-up, but Towle has always suspected it was him.

Bud eventually turned his rage against his family. In 1987, when his younger brother, Stick, accused him of physically abusing their grandfather and taking his money, Bud grabbed him and threw him down the stairs. On December 8, 1987, Christine Brown, suffering from liver disease, told the court that she had fled her home and asked to have her husband removed as well. The elder Alvin Brown died a short time later and Bud's

neighborhood.

"Be on guard, rapist around," "Walk in safety" and "Be cautious" dot the roadside along Southwest Taylors Ferry Road.

The warnings, residents say, are not without foundation.

The area, roughly bounded by

in the area told Portland detectives that last February she received a call from a man who said her son had been in a serious accident. The unidentified man told the woman to meet him at a designated spot and that they would drive to the accident scene. The woman picked the man up, and after driving for a while, the man said there was no accident and that he planned to rape her. The woman fought the man and then ran from the car.

— In May, about a mile from Mrs. Burnett's home, the body of Kimberly Stevens, 17, 1185 S.W. Lesser Road, was discovered in a bushy area behind a church.

— Also in May, the body of Norene Davis, 31, Aloha, was discovered in Tigard. Mrs. Davis was working in a restaurant and lounge in Metzger, near the scenes of other crimes, when she received a call from an unidentified man. Mrs. Davis told a friend at the lounge that the call was from a friend who said he had an accident and couldn't go to the police. She left the lounge about 3 a.m. to meet her friend. Her body was discovered that afternoon next to her car, which was parked along the road.

— In March, a woman who lived in the area received a call from a man who told her that her boyfriend had wrecked his truck and needed a ride. The woman drove to a designated site, but when she saw there was no accident she became scared and drove away.

— In April, a 15-year-old girl walking along Southwest Taylors Ferry

Staff photos by MICHAEL LLOYD

RAPE PROTEST — Signs on telephone poles near Interstate 5's Capitol Highway exit tell the story of a crime problem that has nearby residents worried.

The southwest Portland neighborhood where Bud grew up felt safer when he was in prison. (*Multnomah County Library*)

grandmother after that. The family squabble made its way through probate court, and the brothers became bitterly estranged.

In June 1987, Bud married Jackie Haratyk, the healthcare worker who cared for his grandfather. In her 2019 interview for the tv-program *Evil Lives Here*, Jackie paints a rosy picture of her life with Bud. "He was everything this woman could have wanted," she explained, "It was pretty ideal for me." The truth, however, is that Bud was a master of domination and deception, but Jackie seems to have participated in her own blindness, willfully ignoring the things he did and refusing to acknowledge what was going on. She describes her shock at discovering Bud had been convicted of rape and served time in prison, but she easily shrugged it off when he claimed he had not committed the crime. She tells about her husband's "stone-cold" stare and an odd distance that came over him "once or twice a month" and always preceded an unexplained over-night absence. She explained it to herself as "nights out with the boys" and let it go at that.

Denial helped Jackie Brown cling to a "perfect life" she convinced herself they were leading but finding a hypodermic syringe in her basement was the last straw. Jackie insisted that Bud get into drug rehab and abruptly left for her mother's house in Idaho.

Mike Hefley and Paul Lazenby were not in denial about Bud Brown and his consistently violent behavior. The two homicides detectives, from different departments, had become convinced that Bud was the killer of Kim Stevens, Norene Davis, Melina Crist, and Sheila Burnett. Without physical evidence to connect Bud to the crimes though, there was little they could do other than keeping an eye on him. Periodically keeping watch on his house or his car and collecting stories from other officers who knew Bud or ran into him, Hefley and Lazenby knew it was only a matter of time before he would do it again.

In 1990, technology gave the detectives new hope; scientists had learned to extract DNA from physical evidence and connect crimes to specific individuals. Although Melina Crist's body had been buried too long to leave useable evidence, semen samples found on the bodies of both Stevens and Davis had been preserved. It would take more than a decade, but eventually, Bud Brown was connected to both victims through reliably tested DNA evidence.

In 1991, Sheila Burnett's body, buried for a decade, was discovered in the backyard of a Tigard house. It was the same house Bud Brown rented for a short time in the spring of 1981, when Burnett had disappeared. By this time, Brown was in new legal trouble. Suspected of renting landscaping equipment from two different companies and selling it for profit, the district attorney was close to indicting Brown for larceny. The noose seemed to be tightening, and Brown could see that he would be going back to prison. It was during this time that his wife found the hypodermic needle and finally left him.

There are as many motives for serial killing as there are serial killers. Each killer follows their own dark desire or overwhelming compulsion, but what connects them all is an addiction to killing. The act of taking someone's life has become intoxicating for them. It gives them a rush of power and a feeling of being "in control" that they come to crave. Already addicted to the intravenous drugs that would kill him before the age of sixty after a total of twenty years in prison, Bud Brown began to crave the power that only violence and domination of women could give him.

Brown was deft at crossing jurisdictional lines; each of the four murders he is suspected of was committed in a different police jurisdiction, making it harder for police to connect his crimes or notice discernable patterns. There were several violent crimes against women in and around Portland during the time he was active, and some of them share similar characteristics to Brown's crimes. His final victim survived Brown's attack, but she lost a leg and spent five weeks in a coma after Bud threw her into traffic from a freeway overpass. At least two other women appear to have been thrown from freeway overpasses in the area around Portland that year, a highly unusual crime itself, but no one ever connected Bud to those crimes, if they occurred. Tragically, in all three cases, the female victims were so badly injured they could remember nothing of what happened to them or how they had come to be beneath an overpass.

The September 1991 disappearance of Denyel Dillenburg and Shawn Anderson, two sixteen-year-old Tigard High School students, echoes eerily with Bud's crimes. The girls disappeared after receiving a phone call and leaving to "pick up a friend in Tigard." When they were not back in an hour as they promised, Denyel's mother, Debra Dillenburg, got nervous. She filed a missing person report with the police as soon as she was able. Late in November, the bodies of the two girls were found thrown down a steep embankment in the Mount Hood National Forest. Bud Brown and Douglas Franklin Wright were briefly suspects in the double murder, but they were both eventually ruled out.[2]

Evidence indicates that Bud was spending his "nights out" picking up prostitutes from various "vice districts" around town. Bud acted out the mounting pressure of criminal charges and marital separation with increasingly violent behavior directed against women. In October, shortly after Jackie demanded he enter rehab and walked out, Bud picked up a young woman in Old Town and took her back to his house for sex. As he was driving her back to town, Bud stopped near the S.W. 22nd Avenue overpass, raped the woman, and then pushed her from the moving car as he drove away. Dazed and slightly injured, the woman memorized the licenses plate of Bud's car, repeating it to herself as she limped home where she could write it down.

A few weeks later, Bud was back in Old Town, picking up another young prostitute, Bonnie Bowen (not her real name). Bowen's twin sister, who also worked the streets downtown, saw Bonnie get into a car with Bud. He took Bonnie back to his house and had sex with her. As he was driving her back to town afterward, again near the same freeway overpass, he attacked her, trying to rape her and finally throwing her into the heavy traffic of Interstate-5. Connie Cooper, a truck driver from Redding, CA, stopped traffic with her truck and carried the badly injured young woman across the freeway. Before lapsing into a coma, Bowen told Cooper, "I did everything he wanted and he still hurt me." Bonnie Bowen suffered traumatic memory loss in addition to losing her leg, so she never testified in Bud's trial.[3] Even without the testimony of his last victim, it was clear to see the danger Bud presented to the community, especially to women.

When Detectives Hefley and Lazenby arrested Bud Brown on Thanksgiving Day, 1991, they felt there was enough evidence to put him away for quite a long time, but they still could not charge him with any of the 1981 murders. There were plenty of charges, though: larceny in the rental equipment case; rape, robbery and assault in the October attack; and attempted murder in the first degree for the November attack on Bonnie Bowen.

Bud made one last attempt at domination in the interrogation room, as Mike Hefley tells it. When confronted with the charges and suspicions against him, Bud mocked, "I'm like Hannibal Lecter … that's my favorite movie."[4] He denied everything, and at one point, he grabbed Hefley's necktie, choking him and making the veteran detective fear for his life. "Alvin Brown is the most dangerous man I've ever dealt with," Hefley says, "He was a predator, nothing less. What's worse is that he lived in my neighborhood and I was afraid for my family while he was loose."

Bud Brown received the heaviest penalty the judge could legally give him on the attempted murder charge. Calling Brown "an unusually dangerous offender," Judge Irving Steinbock sentenced him to nearly sixty-nine years in the Oregon Penitentiary. Ten years later, when the DNA evidence from the Stevens and Davis murders matched up, Hefley knew that Bud would never get out of prison and he never did. Bud died of liver disease associated with decades of heavy drug use in 2012.

ENDNOTES

CHAPTER 2

1 See Chapter 1.
2 I tell the story in detail in *Murder and Mayhem in Portland, OR.*
3 *The Oregonian* was not completely off base about the political motivation of Lappeus' accusers. Before the end of the year, it came out that Mayor Chapman had accepted $2,000 from Lucerne Besser to replace Chief Lappeus. I tell the story of Besser's years-long struggle to get control of the police force in my book *Hidden History of Portland*.

CHAPTER 3

1 I tell this story in greater detail in *Hidden History of Portland* and my Weird Portland Blog.
2 I provide more details regarding James Lotan's unusual story in *Hidden History of Portland*.

CHAPTER 4

1 Dave Campbell volunteered with the fire department at the age of fourteen and eventually became a full-time fire fighter. In the 1890s, he served two terms as Portland fire chief, being put out of office during the chaotic term of Mayor Sylvester Pennoyer and held that position until 1911. He became one of the leading fire chiefs in the country and a hero to many Portlanders. He died in 1911 during a conflagration at the Union Oil plant in Southeast Portland. His funeral is still credited as the largest ever held in Portland, and he became a symbol of public service. His memorial, located on West Burnside, recognizes the deaths "in the line of duty" of many Portland first responders.
2 Not to be confused with William Harrison Demspey, "The Manassa Mauler," who was world heavyweight champion from 1919–1926 and became one of the most popular boxers of all time fighting under the name of his childhood hero, Jack Dempsey.
3 See Chapter 3.
4 I tell the story of the killing and trial in *Murder and Mayhem in Portland, Oregon.*

CHAPTER 6

1 See Chapter 9.

CHAPTER 7

1 For a more detailed account of both of these crimes, see my book *Murder and Scandal in Prohibition Portland*.
2 See Chapter 6.

CHAPTER 8

1 Clara Munson was elected mayor of Warrenton in the same election but took office first. Alice E. Burns was elected mayor of Florence in 1895.
2 In 1929, Fred Jalo (real name Albert Nyhus), a World War I veteran from Klamath Falls who suffered from P.T.S.D. and liked to dress as a woman, confessed to a San Francisco court that he was the Blonde Burglar of Portland. In 1932, Nyhus was wrongly sentenced to a life in prison as a "habitual criminal," a verdict that was overturned in 1953.
3 Ironically, Runyon was a court reporter in the Clackamas County court where the hearing in Lucian's divorce from Josephine was heard.
4 Lucian's doctor, who announced his death and refused to answer questions about it, was Portland's most prominent African American physician, Dr. DeNorval Unthank.
5 See *Portland on the Take*.
6 See *Portland on the Take*.

CHAPTER 9

1 Tongs were Chinese-American benevolent, protective societies, some of which engaged in illegal businesses. For more information about tongs, see Chapter 8 and *Murder and Mayhem in Portland, OR*.
2 I tell this story in more detail in *Murder and Scandal in Prohibition Portland*.
3 A community that was destroyed as mercilessly as Albina in the urban renewal of the 1950s and 1960s.
4 The drivers for Tonkin's taxicab combine were all purpose vice-caterers and tough guys. A common tactic among Tonkin's drivers was to call for remote pickups by rival drivers, beat them, and steal their cab. The stolen cab went into an efficient chop-shop system and improved Tonkin's taxi fleet. The driver was blacklisted and essentially banned from taxi-driving in Portland.
5 Johnson once purchased a new pistol for a federal agent who "lost his" while serving a search warrant at one of Johnson's places. Johnson said he did not want the officer to "lose his property while searching mine."
6 To learn about the Vice Scandal, read Phil Stanford's *Portland Confidential* and Robert C. Donnelly's *Dark Rose*.

CHAPTER 10

1 Mikal Gilmore says that Gary and Leroy had been taking pills and went to a Little Richard concert before running out of gas on S.E. 82nd and deciding to steal the car. Little Richard was not in town, so it was more likely the movie *Don't Knock the Rock* or *The Girl Can't Help It*.
2 See Chapter 12.

CHAPTER 11

1 I tell this story in detail in my podcast *Murder by Experts* on podomatic.com.
2 From 1955 to 1958, recording star Willie Nelson was a popular disc jockey on Vancouver, WA, country music radio station K.V.A.N. In 1957, he recorded his first record, a single of his song "No Place for Me," at a Portland recording studio.

3 I tell this story in greater detail in chapter nine and in *Murder and Scandal in Prohibition Portland*.

4 The truth was that the heroin came from Nationalist China (Taiwan) with assistance from the C.I.A. You can read all about it in *The Politics of Heroin* (2003) by Alfred McCoy.

5 George Roy Hill's *The Sting* (1973).

6 I tell this story in more detail in my blogs and in *Murder and Scandal in Prohibition Portland*.

CHAPTER 12

1 See Chapter 10.

2 Viesenback was awarded the Cross of Valor by the Oregon Sheriff's Association for his actions in helping arrest Douglas Wright.

3 To learn about these cases and more about the life of Des Connall read Phil Stanford's books, *The Peyton-Allen Case* and *Rose City Vice*.

4 See Chapter 10.

5 Later, Kitzhaber imposed a complete ban on executions in Oregon that still holds under his successor.

CHAPTER 13

1 In May 1992, the murder of Hal Charbonneau, a disabled Vietnam veteran, led Mike Hefley to Charbonneau's son Grant and a gang of homeless kids who killed several people.

2 See Chapter 12.

3 Years later, Cordes Towle, who was promoted to detective in 1993, saw the twin sisters back working the streets downtown, with Bonnie on crutches.

4 In the 1991 film *The Silence of the Lambs*, Anthony Hopkins played the diabolical serial killer Hannibal Lecter.

BIBLIOGRAPHY

As usual, my main source was *The Oregonian* Historical Archive at the Multnomah County Library, where I can read local daily reporting back to 1861. I also used the facilities of ancestry.com to read census and other public records.

Blalock, B., *Portland's Lost Waterfront: Tall Ships, Steam Mills and Sailors' Boardinghouses* (History Press, Charleston, 2012).

Blalock, B., *The Oregon Shanghaiers: Columbia River Crimping from Astoria to Portland* (History Press, Charleston, 2014).

Blalock, B., *Oregon Prizefighters: Forgotten Bare-knuckle Champions of Portland & Astoria* (History Press, Charleston, 2015).

Carpenter, D., *Hard Rain Falling* (New York Review Books, NY, 1964, 2009).

Chambreau, E., *Biography and Recollections of Edward Chambreau, Oregon Pioneer Compiled by His Son William Wadhams Chambreau* (unpublished) http://chambreauresources.com/ned/life.htm

Chandler, J. D., *Murder and Mayhem in Portland, OR* (History Press, Charleston, 2013).

Chandler, J. D., *Hidden History of Portland, OR* (History Press, Charleston, 2013).

Chandler, J. D. and Fisher, J. B., *Portland on the Take: Mid-Century Crime Bosses, Civic Corruption and Forgotten Murders* (History Press, Charleston, 2014).

Chandler, J. D. and Kennedy. T., *Murder & Scandal in Prohibition Portland: Sex, Vice and Misdeeds in Mayor Baker's Reign* (History Press, Charleston, 2016).

DeMuniz, P. and Gilgan, L., "Sentenced to Death for Life Part 1" oadp.org/paul-de-muniz-essay-sentenced-to-death-for-life (2016).

DeMuniz, P., and Gilgan, L., "Sentenced to Death for Life: Part 2" oadp.org/news/sentenced-to-death-for-life-part-2 (2016).

Dietsche, R., *Jumptown: The Golden Years of Portland Jazz 1942–1957* (OSU Press, Corvallis, 2005).

DuPay, D., *Behind the Badge in River City: A Portland Police Memoir* (Oregon Greystone Press, Portland, 2015).

Lenzen, C., *The Ghost of Thomas G. O'Connor; A Portland, Oregon Policeman* (2006, unpublished).

Karson, L., *American Smuggling as White Collar Crime* (Routledge, New York, London, 2014).

Gilmore, M., *Shot in the Heart.* (Anchor Books, NY, 1994).

"Hammer Murders Author Tells All," *Kitsap Sun*, products.kitsapsun.com/archive/1999/11-06/0052_the_hammer_murders__author_tells_.html

"Haytian Republic" wrecksite.eu/wreck.aspx?283966

Herring, C., "Tent City, America," *Places Journal*, December 2015, placesjournal.org/article/tent-city-america/?gclid=EAIaIQobChMIlozwlqzW5gIVCMZkCh0XQwxzEAAYASAAEgJNNfD_BwE&cn-reloaded=1_

Holbrook, S., *Wildmen, Wobblies and Whistlepunks: Stewart Holbrook's Lowbrow Northwest* (OSU Press, Corvallis, 1992).

"How farm girl turned gangster escaped the noose," *Seattle Post Intelligencer,* seattlepi.com/news/article/How-farm-girl-turned-gangster-escaped-the-noose-1108879.php

John, F., *Wicked Portland: The Wild and Lusty Underworld of a Frontier Seaport Town* (History Press, Charleston, S.C., 2012).

Lansing, J., *Portland: People, Politics and Power 1851-2001* (OSU Press, Corvallis, 2005).

Leeson, F., *Rose City Justice: A Legal History of Portland, OR* (Oregon Historical Society Press, Portland, 1998).

MacColl, E. K., *The Shaping of a City: Business and Politics in Portland 1885-1915* (The Georgian Press, Portland, 1976).

MacColl, E. K., *The Growth of a City: Power and Politics in Portland, OR 1915-1950* (The Georgian Press, Portland, 1979).

MacColl, E. K., *Merchants, Money and Power: The Portland Establishment 1843-1913* (The Georgian Press, Portland, 1988).

Mailer, N., *Executioner's Song* (Grand Central Publishers, New York. 1979).

National Academy of Sciences, "The History of Homelessness in the United States," National Academies Press, July 2018. ncbi.nlm.nih.gov/books/NBK519584/

Prohibition Department Investigation of Tom Johnson *et al.* National Archive and Records Administration, Seattle.

Oregon State Prison Inmate Records: #5239, 5876, 6284, 7903, 8023, 8024, 8025, 8390, 8391, 9505, 9506, 9516, 9517, 9518, 9519, 10097, 11744. *Oregon State Archive,* Salem.

"Rogues Gallery," *Image: Journal of Photography of the George Eastman House,* October 1952, p. 2.

Stanford, P., *Rose City Vice: Portland in the 70s: Dirty Cops and Dirty Robbers* (Feral House, Pt. Townsend, 2017).

Streckert, J., "The Birthplace of Homelessness," *Portland Mercury*, March 16, 2016. portlandmercury.com/feature/2016/03/16/17757826/the-birthplace-of-homelessness

Tracy, C., "Police Function in Portland 1851-1874 Part 1" *Oregon Historical Quarterly,* Vol. LXXX, Spring 1979, pp. 5–29, (Portland, OHS, 1979).

Tracy, C., "Police Function in Portland 1851-1874 Part 2" *Oregon Historical Quarterly,* Vol. LXXX, Summer 1979, pp. 135–169 (Portland, OHS, 1979).

Tracy, C., "Police Function in Portland 1851-1874 Part 3" *Oregon Historical Quarterly,* Vol. LXXX, Fall 1979, pp. 287–322 (Portland, OHS, 1979).